The Year Mom Got Religion

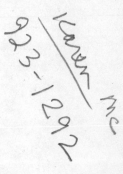

The Year Mom Got Religion

One Woman's Midlife Journey into Judaism

Lee Meyerhoff Hendler

JEWISH LIGHTS PUBLISHING

Woodstock, Vermont

The Year Mom Got Religion
One Woman's Midlife Journey into Judaism

1999 First Quality Paperback Edition

All of the author's royalties from this book will be donated to the adult learning and family education programs at Chizuk Amuno Congregation in Baltimore, Maryland.

Library of Congress Cataloging-in-Publication Data

    Hendler, Lee Meyerhoff, 1952–
    The year mom got religion : one woman's midlife journey into Judaism / by Lee Meyerhoff Hendler.
    p.   cm.
    ISBN 1-58023-000-8 (Hardcover)
    ISBN 1-58023-070-9 (Quality Paperback)
    1. Jewish way of life. 2. Spiritual life–Judaism. 3. Hendler, Lee Meyerhoff, 1952– Religion. 4. Jewish women–Religious life–United States. 5. Judaism–United States. I. Title.
    BM723.H38   1998
    296.7-dc21   98-35464
                CIP

10 9 8 7 6 5 4 3 2 1

Manufactured in the United States of America

Jacket design: Bronwen Battaglia
Text design: Kate Mueller

Published by Jewish Lights Publishing
A Division of LongHill Partners, Inc.
Sunset Farm Offices, Route 4
P.O. Box 237
Woodstock, VT 05091
Tel: (802) 457-4000   Fax: (802) 457-4004

www.jewishlights.com

To my mother, Lenore P. Meyerhoff, my first teacher

" " " , Peggy A. Dean,
(chambers)

Contents

Introduction

Credit for the title of this book goes to my son, Sam, who coined the phrase, and to Ron Wolfson, vice president of the University of Judaism in Los Angeles, who suggested I use it. The suggestion came during a late-night conversation at the Jewish Funders Network Conference in Boston in April 1995. Ron and I had met just hours before. I knew of him from his nationally recognized work as a Jewish family educator and as the author of *The Passover Seder* and other books in The Art of Jewish Living Series (Jewish Lights). He knew of me because we had just met. We liked each other immediately—relishing the easy intimacy that kindred spirits enjoy. I laughed at his stories; he laughed at mine. We shared what we were doing with our lives, what excited and disheartened us. Suddenly, he declared, "You need to write a book about all of this!"

"What are you talking about? What would I put in a book?"

"This," he answered, opening his arms and sweeping them together as if to gather up all the words that had crossed between us in those few hours.

"You don't even know if I can write."

"Anyone who talks the way you do can write."

"And what would you suggest I call it? *Confessions of a* Ba'al Teshuvah [newly Orthodox]?" I mimed a gagging motion. With four kids, I had it down cold.

He chuckled. "No. Nothing that predictable. You'll call it . . . you'll call it . . . what your son called it: *The Year Mom Found Religion!*"

"He called it *The Year Mom Got Religion.*"

"Even better."

"Don't you think that's a bit cute? Doesn't the subject deserve more dignity?"

"Lee, it's *funny!* We're not talking about rabbinic ordination. If we can't keep our sense of humor in all of this then we're taking ourselves far too seriously. There has to be some joy in it!" The last sentence came out as both a plea and a proclamation.

Just What the World Needs . . . Another Self-Help Book

Joy! He'd used my favorite word. Earlier that year, a fellow synagogue board member, a psychiatrist with a sharp wit and even sharper tongue, had dubbed me "The Queen of Joy" because I kept trying to insert the word into a congregational mission statement we were drafting. I believe that joy and learning are synonymous. Ron's bid for joy recast the challenge. Writing a book might be a way to share with others some of the joy I have experienced. A serious good news book rather than another maudlin confessional memoir: the possibility excited me. Contrary to what the title may imply, this is really not a year-long chronological narrative. Instead, it covers four years of my life from ages forty to forty-four, the period during which I gradually awakened to the beauty of Judaism and began the rewarding process of incorporating it into my life. I've tried to capture my growth over those few years without denying my history. I don't believe that like some Greek god's spontaneous offspring, I suddenly sprang forth fully formed and ready for religion at age forty. Like all human beings, since the moment I became conscious I have lived in a state of readiness for religion. The need to acknowledge and understand that readiness, however, only became a passion when I reached that classic midlife milestone—a confluence I prefer to call a midlife growth spurt, not a midlife crisis. I became committed to writing about it when I discovered that other adult Jews shared this same passion and that many more were beginning to cautiously probe the nature of their Jewish identities.

At the same time, I was traveling around the country speaking to Jewish audiences about the issues of intergenerational philanthropy, an emerging national concern and an area in which I have an expertise based on personal experience. What surprised me was the interest from audiences in hearing less philanthropic theory and more personal reflection. They seemed almost starved for it, with question-and-answer sessions often exceeding the allotted time; business cards thrust on me at the close of a program with requests for anything I'd written that related to Judaism; the occasional phone call from a stranger: "I heard you when you were in New York and I was wondering if you would be willing to talk to my daughter who wants to send her children to day school. She's afraid of what this might do to her relationship with her husband."

It was fine to talk in the abstract about conveying values across generations, but how was I doing it in my own family? It was worth stating that we needed a higher degree of Jewish literacy in the adult community if we wanted knowledgeable Jewish philanthropists, but how was I pursuing my *own* education? If a solid childhood Jewish education was so important to Jewish identity, what choices had I made for my own children? It was nice to claim that I had been transformed in the past few years, but *exactly* what did that mean in real life terms? It was interesting to talk about the failure of ethnic Judaism, but was I actually suggesting that Jews needed to start getting serious about Judaism as a *religion?* And most significantly, because it seemed to reflect others' greatest fears and anxieties, how had the change I had undertaken affected my own family, my relationships with the people I loved most in the world?

Good-bye, Soccer Mom . . . Hello, Mrs. Akiva!

Apparently, the value was not so much in the message itself but in the messenger's experience. Jewish audiences had been ignoring messengers bearing many of the same messages for years. Now, however, they seemed ready and able to listen—not only because the timing was right, but because the messenger came from their ranks and understood their lives in a way no "professional" could. My credentials as a peer were telegraphed through my dress, my vocabulary, my history and my characterization of our collective American Jewish experience. The questions I encountered were never hostile, rarely confrontational. People were not throwing down the gauntlet, but doing just the opposite: inviting me into their communities and their lives with open arms, grace and generosity. What was striking was the hunger not for answers per se, but for possibilities and, most importantly, for honesty.

The audiences I addressed weren't interested in blithe prescriptions for their Jewish health unless I was willing to testify to my own experience with the same over-the-counter preparations. They were suspicious of nonchalance and pressed hard when I appeared to downplay the difficulties or complexity of what I had undertaken. They were after the guts, the inside of the process that had brought me to them. Intuitively, they grasped that religious transformation was not simple and I finally understood that clarity about my own story was helping them discover what it might mean to "get" religion—more specifically what it means to "get" the religion that is *in* Judaism.

I don't think that Sam, my oldest child, intended multiple meanings when he came up with the phrase, "The Year Mom Got Religion." He was trying to reduce the experience to its essence, and summoning a comical image of tambourines and revival meetings did the trick for him. When I first heard him say it, I laughed because he so aptly captured the intensity of what I had done—in terms of what it meant to me *and* to my family. I had a new passion and because I'm a Mom, my family suddenly had a different Mom. This was a life-changing event for all of us. Although the changes felt slow and deliberate to me, the process must have seemed precipitous and occasionally calamitous to them. One day they had a soccer Mom, the next day they were living with "Mrs." Akiva. It was a tectonic shift: my new life was heaving up over my old one.

From the beginning, it was clear to all of us that there was no turning back. But to stop there was to oversimplify a very complicated process. Something was *missing* if I accepted Sam's introductory statement as the final summation, as a "Hallelujah, I have been saved!" story. That was certainly where I started, in the sense that I delighted in discovering the beauty and richness of Judaism each day, and felt a childlike wonder at being able to give myself up to all I was learning and doing. But to end the story there suggested the wrong-headed belief that if only I was desirous enough and well-intentioned enough, religion was something I could go out and *get*, like a bag of groceries. Or something I could *receive,* like a birthday present. I sensed the need for a construct more rigorous and demanding of me—and of my tradition. And now, some four years later, I have a more satisfactory explanation.

I was "getting" all the trappings of religious practice, steadily and persistently acquiring the skills that would enable me to participate more fully as an adult citizen in my Jewish community. But what I was "getting" much more deeply, and with a great deal more difficulty, was the purpose of religion itself. I was beginning to understand the role of religion in our lives, the reasons we need it and, on a personal level, the reasons I required a coherent system of religious practice and belief in my life. I have known since childhood that we all have our Jewish stories to tell. It's impossible to emerge from the American Jewish experience without knowing that. The more powerful understanding was realizing that we Jews *all* have our religious stories to tell, *whether or not we think we believe in religion.* We are all searching for meaning in our lives. The existential questions of a conscious being—"What is the meaning of life?" and "Why am I here?"—must be answered. Whatever system we turn to for answers *becomes our religion* whether we call it that or not. We organize our lives around that system and create rituals to mark and reinforce our belief in it. This book is about "getting" what a religion with God at its center can mean in our lives: How turning to a system that has divine, not human, authority as its cornerstone can bring order and purpose to bear on our significant decisions and choices, and how that meaning can influence who we are and want to be. Henry James once wrote, "Nature loves chaos and man loves order." If that is true, then I have found that Judaism has the remarkable capacity to help me order my existence by offering particularly persuasive and enduring answers to those universal existential questions. Judaism orients and stabilizes me as I face the chaotic world around me. A moral compass, it constantly displays the crucial coordinates of right and wrong, indignation and indifference, providing essential bearings for my conduct and ongoing development. For me, venturing out into the world without it any longer is equivalent to plunging into an unknown wilderness on a cloudy night without a real compass, choosing to depend instead on random signs and cues for survival.

In writing this book, I have ignored the advice of Shammai, a great (but cranky) sage of Jewish tradition, who in *Pirke Avot, The Sayings of Our Fathers,* enjoins us to "Make your Torah [study] a habit; *say little and do much;* and greet every person cheerfully." Once I decided to say a lot, I had to make choices about what to withhold and what to share. Those choices were all governed by the desire to instruct rather than entertain. The instructional value, I hope, is not through representing myself as the teacher, which I'm not, but as the *student:* eager, impatient, hungry, overwhelmed, self-centered, humbled, egotistical, self-congratulatory, enchanted, frustrated and finally completely in love with Judaism.

I have tried to be faithful to those friends, teachers and relatives portrayed in this book. I briefly considered trying to preserve their anonymity, but quickly discovered that I am not a mystery writer. My initial efforts to camouflage identities were at best transparent, at worst insulting. It somehow seemed fairer and cleaner this way. I have also tried to be honest about my own feelings, thoughts and actions. We all have a tendency to want to put our best foot forward when we step out before the public eye. My problem is that I have flat feet. Since all the clumsy, corrective shoes of my childhood failed to correct this congenital flaw, I still step out into the world putting one flat foot after another, wanting to believe that others aren't looking at my feet so much as where they are taking me. Some might consider this assumption charming but improbably naive. The truth is that it is as much a part of me as my feet, so I take responsibility for living with the consequences of holding to it. Most of all, I pray that *The Year Mom Got Religion* will encourage others to step out as well, flat feet or no, and that somewhere along the way readers will smile, learn and know joy.

8/30/18

1

Bereshit or Beginnings:
Every Story Has to Have One

The love of parents goes to their children,
but the love of these children goes to their children.

—Talmud, *Sotah* 49a

At first, the recollections present themselves as fragments, disorganized and unassembled. I seek the source of my present in my past. I want to get at the core of my childhood Jewish identity. What was it made of? How did I construct it? How was it conveyed to me and by whom? If I can't answer these questions then I can't successfully rearrange and assemble my adult Jewish identity—the goal I am after. I have to know where I've been in order to know where I'm going. I know I must have plenty of Jewish moments in my history; I just never had any reason to examine them closely or mark them as particularly noteworthy. So I set out to find all the pieces and put them together. It's not like Humpty Dumpty. I'm not putting them together *again.* I'm putting them together *for the first time.* There's a great temptation to falsify the records, to make the story into a charming fairy tale. Like everyone else, I prefer my stories tidy and compact with a definite beginning, a solid middle and a happy end. But I know I should resist the temptation. The real story with all of its untidiness will probably be more interesting. I have to take the story as it comes because that's the way life works. This is what comes when I first begin to remember.

I knew we were Jewish because we spent every Friday night together as a family. My first recollections of Shabbat are jumbled and remote. Nothing definitive jumps out until an image suddenly looms before me—so clear and alive I can almost touch it. I'm dozing in the back of my parents' car, a '57 fin-tailed whale of a Cadillac that sailed me home every Friday night after dinner at my grandparents' house. I loved the drowsy comfort of that car ride, the smell of leather by my cheek, the lingering scent of roast chicken still on my fingertips. As I lay back against the seat, lulled by the car's solid momentum and the familiar cadence of my parents' quiet adult talk, I would replay the evening in my head.

The table laden with fancy china, sparkling crystal, gleaming silver candlesticks and bright candles offered an elegant counterpoint to the unrelenting conversational barrage. You had to be quick as a cheetah and strong as a bull in our family. Stop for a breath or a pause and an interloper rudely seized the opportunity to finish your sentence for you or to send the conversation careening off in another direction. There was only one rule: No business at the table. It was a serious rule for a family that did all of its business together. I didn't learn much about patience at that table, and I certainly didn't learn anything about business, but I learned a lot about dominance, timing, drama and endurance.

On this particular evening, I had been offered the much-coveted privilege of climbing onto Grandma's lap after dinner to flip open the cover of her special gold wristwatch. This was a "by invitation only" activity. You had to be asked by Grandma and you were allowed to do it no more than three times in a row. More than that might "break" it. I always savored my three chances, lingering for as long as Grandma might tolerate me. The strangest thing is that this wasn't a ritual we created: it was one she invented. No one ever wondered about her watch until she introduced us to it. For a woman with little imagination and even less patience for small, wriggling children, it was a brilliant bid for attention. For that instant, she was the most alluring human being in the world, eclipsing our laughing parents, our baseball-throwing grandfather and our irrepressible Uncle Jack. It was basically the only time we dealt with her other than to ask her permission to enter certain rooms, to leave the table or to touch certain things. When my turn was over, she gave me and my little sister, Jill, permission to enter her dressing room, the closest thing to sacred space in her home. In awe, we stood before her open closet doors and gazed at the miraculous order revealed there. Tiny shoes in tissue packed carefully in stacked plastic box towers, layers of sweaters folded in individual plastic slipcovers, handbags lined up in daytime and evening rows, fancy dresses hung on specially padded hangers in zippered cloth bags. All the hangers even faced the same direction. Watching her closet was almost better than watching TV, and it was fully sanctioned by Grandma. She was so proud of her closets and her immaculate home! She probably hoped some of her domestic discipline would rub off on us. To her, the daughter of poor immigrants, order was a virtue; taking care of fine things was a supreme privilege and an obligation. To us, the third-generation descendants of those immigrants—materially pampered baby boomers—it was an amusing spectator sport, but not something we felt compelled to imitate. Poor Grandma. If she could see my closets and front hall today she'd never let me on her lap again.

Once again, my older sister, Terry, and my cousin, Richie, played hide-and-seek with us and terrified us at the top of the basement stairs. Our excited shrieks drew the expected adult reaction, "No more screaming!" Giggling, we scurried up to the guest bedroom suite on the second floor to play with the grooming aids laid out on the fancy, silk-skirted dressing table and to make silly faces in the mirror. The games, the conversations, the routines all tumbled together in my head and body, a messy mixture of rich sights, raucous sounds and pleasant tastes. I hungrily devoured the experience whole each week, but it wasn't until I climbed into that solid Cadillac each night that it began to digest, slowly seeping into my consciousness as I drifted off to sleep. This is what Shabbat meant to me as a five-year-old: a safe place to sleep after a safe place to eat. A place to gather myself together, a place to start from as I began to figure out who I was in the world and how that came to be.

Crucifixes, Curses and Circumcisions

I knew we were Jewish because we did not respond to the church bells that rang out every Sunday morning. The sound carried over the ridge of the rural valley we lived in just like the distant whistle of the daily freight train and the muted fire bell of the local fire station, but I knew there was a difference. The train whistle was a call to work, the fire bell to help. This sound was a call to worship. I lay in my bed on Sunday mornings and tried to sing at the same pitch as that church bell, but I always missed. As I hummed my off-tune match, I visualized people streaming into a vaulted space, wearing solemn faces, kneeling down in front of the only image I associated with Christianity: that sad man dangling from those two crossed boards. I knew his name was Jesus. I knew our housekeeper, Carrie, whom I adored and whose velvety arms I loved to burrow into, believed in him because he gave her her brown skin and me my white skin and "he must have known what he was doin' when he did it. Otherwise, I'd be white and you'd be brown." I knew that Jesus was supposed to have some relationship to God and that relationship had something to do with Christmas. I knew that people who believed in him went to church whenever the church bells rang. I knew that we didn't believe in him, but I also knew that we hardly ever went to synagogue.

I knew I was Jewish because the little boy who lived across the street from us stood on his side of the road one day and hurled a fistful of gravel at me while screaming in a high-pitched voice, "Kike! Kike! Kike!" I didn't want to play with him anymore at all, although that was the reason why I had come all the way to the end of our driveway. Now I wanted to throw the gravel back at him, rush across the street and grind his dirt-streaked, grinning little face into the pile of stones he was so righteously heaving at me. I wanted to hurt him the way he had hurt me, throwing names I didn't understand and objects I did. But I didn't do any of those things because I wasn't old enough to cross the street yet by myself. Some rules I did understand.

I knew I was Jewish because when I was five and a half a momentous event occurred in our family. After having three girls, my mother gave birth to a baby boy. This disrupted the pattern of our lives even as it established a new one. Not only was there a stranger living in our house—a crisply dressed nurse who stood guard at his nursery door—but a sense of closure had come to live with us as well. The quality of watchful expectation that had always characterized our family disappeared. Whatever we had been waiting for had finally arrived. This idea was confirmed when eight days after Joe's birth adult relatives and friends streamed into our house. They had come to gather at his *"bris,"* something I'd never heard of but I knew was important because my mother slicked our hair back with styling gel and dressed us in our Florence Eiseman look-alike sister dresses and all the adults were wearing fancy clothes in the daytime. The air was charged with a curious mixture of anxiety and joy, anticipation and reluctance. It seemed to me that whatever was about to happen was irreversible, possibly unpleasant and required witnessing.

Soon, the stern nurse who was taking care of my brother brought him down into the living room where he was passed around like a valuable piece of jewelry. In an apparently preordained game of hot potato, he finally landed in his godfather's lap, our "Uncle" Marvin. Dr. Louis L. Kaplan, my grandfather's teacher and our family's religious leader, stood next to Uncle Marvin and spoke in his sonorous, authoritative voice, teaching as he spoke. I watched the adults listen attentively and respectfully. Then Dr. Kaplan dipped the tip of a diaper in wine and tenderly slipped the makeshift nipple into my brother's mouth. Another man stepped forward, a stranger dressed in a funny white jacket, and the room suddenly achieved the atmospheric pressure of a theater just before the curtain rises. The momentary hush was interrupted almost immediately by the outraged squall of my brother, followed by a surge of nervous adult laughter. I caught one last glimpse of Joe before he was carried away, sucking frantically on the diaper protruding from his mouth while a startled expression blew his eyes wide open on his tiny face.

I roamed the room happily for the next half hour—nuzzling up to the kind touch of people who knew me, sniffing in the exciting air of celebration. Secretly, I couldn't wait to get a look at Joe to see what had happened to him. I also wanted to examine the ornate silver menorah Uncle Marvin had presented to my parents at some point in the ceremony. It looked like the lion heads might lift up on tiny hinges. I wondered what was inside of them.

Taboos and Other Tales

I knew I was Jewish because almost all my friends were Jewish. It wasn't anything we ever talked about. We took it for granted in the same way that we accepted the fact that we all had two parents, two cars, a nice house and household help, and went to The Park School. This was primarily due to the fact that all of Baltimore's private schools still had quotas for Jews and wouldn't even consider enrolling blacks. Our school had been founded in 1912 by a group of Jewish men who had failed to reform the public school system, and resented the private school quota system that excluded most of their children. They decided to create a coeducational school open to children of all religions, dedicated to the principles of the Progressive movement in education. By 1959, The Park School had become the first private school in Baltimore to accept blacks and had moved to a brand new facility, on an expansive 100-acre site. Because prejudice was so firmly entrenched in Baltimore, Park was identified as the "Jewish" private school from the start, despite its founders' admirable democratic intentions.

There were twenty-five children in my second grade class. Maybe five were not Jewish. Instinctively, I knew that *they* were the ones who were different from *us,* but I vowed I would never be unkind to them in the way the little boy across the street had been to me. I sought them out and deliberately cultivated a friendship with one of the Christian boys. He had a dazzling vocabulary filled with words I had never heard before. They sounded dangerous. His favorite rhymed with "duck" and he taught me a funny song about it one day at recess. He forgot to tell me it was a private children's song, the kind you don't repeat to adults. I could barely contain my delight over my newly learned ditty and sang it loudly and proudly as soon as I climbed into my mother's car that afternoon. The grim line of her mouth and the set of her neck instantly affirmed that I'd made a serious mistake.

"Where did you learn that song?"

"On the playground."

"Who taught it to you?"

This posed a fleeting ethical dilemma. If I squealed on Richard, he might get in trouble. If I didn't, I'd be in even worse shape. "Richard taught me. But I didn't know it was bad. I don't even think Richard thought it was bad."

"You get your mouth washed out with soap when we get home. And I never want to hear that word from you again."

With the penalty for my transgression imposed, I regained a bit of my courage. "But, Mommy, what does it *mean?*" After she explained, I was sure I wouldn't want to use the word again until I was a very old lady. I was also sure of another thing. I was different from Richard and he was different from me. Apart from gender, the biggest difference was that he was a Christian and I was a Jew. The difference could get us both into a lot of trouble.

I knew I was Jewish because when my little sister asked me and two of her friends to participate in her private renaming ceremony I understood I was doing something clandestine and I felt guilty. She had decided to change her name from Jill to Sue and to mark her transformation with a special ritual of her own invention. It involved a bowl of water, a red piece of cloth laid across the floor of her closet, a few specially shaped rocks, several incantations and a declaration derived from the civil marriage ceremony: "I now pronounce you 'Sue'!"

At age eight, my sister was precociously playing with ritual. She had divined a power in it that the rest of us had not yet begun to fathom. We obediently followed her directives, intrigued and confused at once. How did she acquire the confidence to know what she wanted to do, what she needed to do? Where did she glean the bits and pieces of this patchwork ceremony that was equal parts pagan and organized religion? It was exciting, but afterwards I was filled with regret and nagging fear. The only thing I knew for sure was that it wasn't Jewish. I had willingly taken part in a taboo activity. I was worried that we had violated some sacred law and that we would get caught and punished for our sins. I discovered at age nine that I was not cut out for New Age religion. I knew instead that I was irrevocably Jewish. And Jews, I was certain, did not hold secret naming ceremonies in closets.

Just the year before this episode, I had begun Sunday school at Baltimore Hebrew Congregation, the largest Reform congregation in Baltimore. Classes were large. From the start, I knew I was like the other students because we were all Jews. But I also felt different from them. Most of the children attended public, not private school. Most lived intense neighborhood lives: they did everything to-gether—eating, playing, going to school—in large, roving neighbor-hood bands. Because of Baltimore's codified housing restrictions, almost all Jews lived in exclusively Jewish neighborhoods. Living in the constant company of other Jews and conducting almost all of their daily business with them, these kids knew things about Jewish community that I couldn't begin to understand. But because my par-ents had opted out of Jewish neighborhood life, I knew things about independence and self-sufficiency that my Sunday school classmates had not yet explored. They knew nothing of my country solitude, how it required me to invent my own entertainment and find daily pleasure in my own company. They seemed to barely tolerate school, it was something they *had* to do in order to get something else they wanted. But I loved school and couldn't wait to get there each day! I loved the excitement of an unanswered question hang-ing in the air. I loved the prickles on my arm when I thought of a new idea or mastered a new skill. I think I loved the idea of learning even more than the act of learning. If anything was sacred in my young life, learning was it.

So as I rushed off to Sunday school for the first time, I was pre-pared to consume everything they offered. It was my first educa-tional disappointment. The teacher didn't want to be there and the kids didn't, either. Besides, the teacher didn't teach us. She ha-rangued us, goaded us, attempted to stuff information into us. This introduced an unfamiliar tension into the classroom—a sense that the teacher was in one place and the students in another. We were not partners in this venture, which violated the rules of the student-teacher relationship I experienced at Park. The violation made Sun-day school boring and emotionally stifling from the start. I didn't hate going but I didn't look forward to it the same way that I eagerly anticipated going to Park School every day.

The only time Sunday school got interesting was in art and music. I loved our art projects because we were free to choose the materials and our projects. I spent weeks on a set of bookends for my cherished collection of medical biographies. Made from un-stained pine, they bore the Hebrew letter *shin*—for *"Shalom"*—that I'd painstakingly shaped out of colored gravel. I carefully sanded all the rough edges away, ran my fingers up and down the warm, smooth planes, and thrilled at the new texture I had created. I used them for years afterwards. In music, I responded happily to the teacher's enthusiastic instruction. Who could resist when joy was present? My favorite melody was "Rock of Ages." It was so special I even sang it in the bathtub.

I knew I was Jewish because every Saturday morning, a delivery man dropped off our weekly delicatessen order from Edmart's Deli-catessen in Pikesville. My father loved tongue and my mother loved smoked fish. I loved corned beef and well-done pickles. I knew that Jews ate their corned beef with rye bread and mustard and that non-Jews had the terrible misfortune to eat theirs with mayo on white bread. We all loved the mouthwatering combination of Nova Scotia lox, cream cheese and Swiss cheese served on bagels. It was our spe-cial Jewish treat. Apart from Grandma's roast chicken and matzah, these were the only foods I ever exclusively associated with being Jewish. Jewish delicatessen became inextricably bound up with the lazy, seductive freedom of weekends—the prospect of unscheduled time I could fill with my favorite activities. The involuntary salivary response that a dill pickle triggered was symbolic of the real need I had to control my own schedule for some part of each week. In the associative leap that maybe only food can enable, I linked being Jew-ish with being free. A refrigerator full of Jewish food was the gate-way to a weekend full of freedom and choices.

I knew I was Jewish because my year derived a secondary rhythm from the rise and fall of a few Jewish holidays and festivals. They acquired a seasonal association in my head that helped regulate the flux and flow of time. Rosh Hashanah and Yom Kippur meant that autumn had arrived along with new school and dress-up clothes. Chanukah signaled winter. More than any other holiday, Chanukah reminded me of our "other" status in America. We sang Christmas songs at school but we got Chanukah presents at home. We couldn't celebrate the "real" holiday that commanded America's nearly undivided attention for almost a month. We had to pass on Christmas trees and Christmas carols, gay lights and lawn decorations, Santa Claus and chestnuts roasting on an open fire. I was always grateful for the wonderful presents I received and fully aware of my parents' delight in giving them. But the nightly ritual of gift-giving never fully compensated for the sense of isolation and inferiority that arose from having to stand on the sidelines as the rest of America vigorously celebrated this national rite. Somehow, eight nights of gifts always felt like the runner-up consolation prize.

8/30/18

The *Shofar* Is Not a Church Bell

Passover heralded spring. The *seder* was hands down my favorite Jewish event. I loved the choreography of it. I loved gathering around the table for a "controlled conversation" that was completely different from the spontaneous cacophony of our other family events. Everyone had a role in this script and we had to make sure we played our assigned parts. Grandpa presided with genuine delight and gentle authority as he looked out over this rambunctious, unmanageable group: "Okay everyone just settle down now. Just settle down." My father would call Grandpa "Pop" more often than usual. This gave me the idea that as long as our parents are alive, we are always their children. When we reached the part in the *Haggadah* that listed the questions of the four kinds of sons, the wise child's question invariably fell to me. I liked that because it was the role I played in real life. It seemed particularly just that I didn't have to audition for the part. Eventually, this bizarre coincidence became part of family lore, so much so that when one year the reading fell to another child, she deferred to me. Invariably, Uncle Jack would tease the youngest children and say he saw Elijah coming up the walk or sneaking around behind the house. Once he even convinced my boisterous little brother, Joe, to sit quietly on the outside front step for close to half an hour while everyone snickered inside. We

always made a big fuss over the reading of the Four Questions. I remember my anxiety and the thrill of accomplishment I felt when the
chanting fell to me for the first time—a privilege I reluctantly relin-
quished two years later when it was my sister's turn to take over. At
dessert, we all joined in loudly proclaiming Grandma's sponge cake
the lightest, finest, most delectable sponge cake in the world. She
bent her head slightly, then beamed her famous photogenic smile in
gracious acknowledgment of our praise. Finally, my mother led us in
an almost bawdy rendition of *"Chad Gadya"* singing in her boom-
ing, brassy voice. She bastardized the refrain of each verse to sound
like "Haddi, gaddi, yaawh—haaaddi, gaaddi, yaaaaaw!!" and set an im-
possibly fast pace for the rest of us to match. We usually drew up
breathless at the end while she, with her swimmer's lungs, could
have held out for at least another full run-through. I did not understand the closing proclamation—"Next year in Jerusalem!"—so in my
head I substituted Baltimore as the evening came to a close. That was
the only place I could ever imagine wanting to be, and a year seemed
an awfully long way off.

We didn't celebrate a Jewish holiday that announced summer's
imminence, but school's end and the relaxing of schedules and time
constraints were more than sufficient. Friday night dinners created
the predictable weekly backdrop against which our clan gathered to
acknowledge our connectedness. I knew that, in some way, being
Jewish imposed order on the world, and gave me a way to make
sense of my place in it. But I understood it only as a minor influence—not as an entire system for grounding and organizing behavior
and belief.

Synagogue was most notable for its conspicuous absence in our
family's Jewish life. When we did go, it seemed more like an unpleasant obligation. We put on our new fall clothes and dutifully
trudged off to worship for the High Holy Days. But we rarely attended services any other time. As we grew older, we stopped going
altogether, and my father conducted Rosh Hashanah services at
home. We each selected readings or made other relevant contributions. I remember my surprise when President Kennedy was assassi-
nated and my mother called from out of town to tell my older sister

to take me with her to synagogue. I was stunned to see a huge crowd there. Synagogue was so devalued as an institution by my parents that I did not know it was a place for community to gather during crisis. Showing up in an emergency confused me.

In truth, I didn't understand why everyone disliked being in synagogue so much, but I quickly learned to enjoy staying home as much as they did. The few times I was in synagogue as a young child seemed peaceful and pleasant enough. I liked being with so many families we knew. It made me feel that we belonged there. I liked the way the sun streamed down from the windows set high in the wall. Whenever a shaft of sunlight, sparkling with dust particles, touched my head, I'd pretend I'd been kissed by God. I liked the color of the wood inside the sanctuary, somewhere between honey and gray tree bark. It felt like the right color for worship: organic, not man-made. I liked to watch the flickering eternal flame set in its rich florentined-gold vessel. Sometimes I wondered what would happen if it went out. Would the rabbi stop everything, find a ladder and strike a match to relight it? Would we have to perform some obscure mass group ritual or say a special prayer? How could we be sure it would never go out? After all, accidents happen. In synagogue, I let my mind roam over all these possibilities. I didn't think God would mind. Maybe God would even think it funny that a small child should worry about such problems. Maybe God would be amazed that a small child could even *think* of such problems.

I always stopped thinking when the ark was opened. I could only stare. I loved the careful way people handled the scrolls. It made me believe they contained very important information. I delighted in the bell-like music the jangling breastplates made when they were lifted or moved. I liked to gaze at the beautiful needlework of the scroll covers and imagine all the work that went into their crafting. I conjured medieval images of ladies in long gowns sitting in rows of straight chairs, patiently lifting their needles in and out, in and out in lovely synchronization, stitching a continuous story of devotion to God and the Jews. I didn't really listen when the Torah portions were read. The words were not important to me, especially since I didn't understand the language. The only thing that mattered were the sights and the sounds of ritual.

The most vivid early sight and sound was the blowing of the *shofar* (ram's horn) on Rosh Hashanah. The first time I heard it I thought of the church bells that sang to me every Sunday morning. But the second blast blew the church bells right out of my head. This sound was a command, the other was a suggestion. With its coarse, primitive notes, the *shofar* was an irrefusable summons to action while the well-tuned bells seemed to be a genteel invitation to assemble. The difference reached across the millennia and yanked me into the drama of the Jewish people. I couldn't explain why, but the raw, plaintive sound of the *shofar* told me I was a Jew. I didn't really know what that meant yet, but the undeniable tug in my gut signaled that it was what I was meant to be.

As I sifted through the artifacts of my Jewish beginnings, these were the memories that came back first. They don't tell the whole story, but they tell an important part of it. As either repeated or one-time moments, each of these experiences shaped my understanding of Judaism without my necessarily knowing it at the time. They got under my skin, into my blood and invaded my psyche because they affected how I *felt*, giving me knowledge I couldn't necessarily articulate at the time. On the affective level, we know things we cannot say. That does not make the knowledge any less valuable, although the biases of modern western thought do deeply discount its value. Affective experience is certainly more difficult to quantify, analyze and understand because its primary cues are non-verbal and it triggers deep, involuntary physical and emotional responses which, of course, are the sources of its lasting power.

My strongest earliest Jewish memories, the ones I can most readily retrieve, are the ones that worked that way. I remember the sights, the smells, the textures, the feelings, the sensations associated with these events *first* because that's how the events registered with me first at the time. Only from the vantage point of adulthood could I begin to break the events down and understand them. Looking back was the perspective I needed to *see* them.

Teasing these memories out from among other childhood memories was surprisingly difficult, though. They were dwarfed by other

activities that elicited greater parental approbation and encouragement. I can readily recall hundreds of athletic exploits, school adventures, artistic achievements, family dinners and discussions,
cultural experiences and vacations. The sparseness of my Jewish
memories does not indicate an underdeveloped capacity for recol-
lection; it simply reflects my family's true priorities. Judaism wasn't
unimportant. It just wasn't *as* important as all the other things we
did. I knew my parents cared about being Jewish, but they often had
a careless attitude toward it. The Jewish moments in our life were
usually fun but seldom serious. They didn't command our reverence
or earn our sustained attention. Most striking, there was an almost
total absence of affection for our tradition. Children learn what and
how to love by seeing what their parents choose to love. I didn't
learn to love Judaism from watching my parents. I learned to be
proud of being Jewish, but my pride had a defiant, sometimes am-
bivalent edge to it: the byproduct of a taught vigilance that was either defensive or preemptive. I learned to protect Judaism, but not
to treasure it. How can a child learn to *properly* protect a thing she
has never been taught to cherish?

2

Bereshit Again: Or, Sometimes a Story Has *Two* Beginnings

Do not separate yourself from the community.

—Hillel, *Pirke Avot* II:5

8/31/18

One day while riding in the car alone with my mother, I asked, "Why is it important to be Jewish?"

"Why do you ask?" she responded.

"I'm just wondering why it's so important for you and Daddy to be Jewish. To see if those would be good reasons for me, too."

I was twelve years old and beginning to make more conscious choices about who I wanted to be. This was the kind of question my mother loved and I knew it: one that addressed the juncture of belief and practice. She readily answered my question with a confidence and conviction that surprised me.

"It's important to me because I feel an obligation to continue what was started over 5,000 years ago. I am a part of that history. So is Daddy. So are you. Also, Judaism is about laws and how people can live together in a community with respect for one another in order to do good things."

So far so good.

"And Israel. It's important to have a place to go where we will always be welcome."

I was beginning to get confused. Was Judaism a reaction against something else? Was Judaism supposed to be a kind of refuge? A place to retreat from reality? My mother took a long breath and spit

15

out the next words as if containing them any longer would cause her physical pain.

"And the Holocaust. We owe it to the millions who died just because they were Jews. We can't let their deaths be meaningless. We have to be Jews because Hitler took that choice away from them. We can never let anyone take that choice from us again. We can't let him win in the end."

Now I was really confused. The reasons were getting all mixed up in my head. Someone, some poor Jew, had died somewhere in Europe, a hapless victim of the Nazi regime. And I was obligated to live my life to honor the memory of that person? A living memorial to the lost options of a dead person? So *many* to remember! Were there enough Jews to go around? How would Hitler know that we had *won?* He was dead already. I couldn't translate these ideas into words at the time. I simply felt trapped by the conflicting emotions they evoked: the swirling eddies of pride, obligation, respect, defensiveness, grief, revenge, guilt. How could these things together constitute a good reason for being Jewish? For me, the answer was a heretic thought: *They might not.* I looked at my mother and said, "I understand what you are saying. The 5,000 years and the laws make sense to me. But I don't think the last two do."

She looked at me with a gentle, loving expression. "That's because you're so young. As you get older, they'll make sense to you too."

I answered, "Maybe." But I thought, "Maybe not."

I had my reasons for the "maybe not." A few weeks before, my parents had returned from a United Jewish Appeal mission to Eastern Europe and Israel. They told wondrous stories of the energy and excitement they had seen in Israel. They marveled at the ashes-to-redemption drama they had witnessed: the Jewish People had ultimately defied Hitler's master plan. I knew of the Holocaust: I had read John Hershey's *The Wall* and *The Diary of Anne Frank*. After seeing the film based on her diary, I even developed a fear of the strange-sounding European police siren that announced the beginning of their end. For months afterwards, that siren punctuated my dreams or screamed in my head. Still, my notion of the Holocaust was essentially a childish one of terrible disruption: the loss of home, school, familiar and comforting routines. I did not yet understand it as an assault on every assumption I felt confident making about human behavior. It would take pictures to do that: silent pictures that carried a horror in their grainy images which I had never conceived of.

Wherever Auschwitz Appears Innocence Departs

My parents brought home a book that catalogued the atrocity of Auschwitz in unflinching detail. Although the early 1960s marked the start of a more serious and widespread effort to document the Holocaust, it was still rare to come across Holocaust visuals in public. They remained largely a private matter. I don't think my parents intended for me to see the book, but it was lying on the desk in their room when I wandered in one day. Attracted by its stark black-and-white cover, I picked it up.

I was a reasonably worldly child. I knew people were capable of all sorts of things. But no worldliness could hold me upright in the tempest I was about to encounter. As I opened the book and saw the first horrific image, something inside me shifted and slipped away. It was the nakedness that undid me first. I saw bodies in flesh sheaths, piled in crumpled heaps, pointed in crazy, impossible angles at gray skies. I saw shriveled, flaccid male genitals set off by pelvic frames that strained at their translucent skin covers. I saw women cowering to escape the humiliation of their public nudity, clamping their arms to their chests, vainly shielding their pubes with one hand while gathering terrified children to the comfort of their bare breasts with the other. I saw rows and rows of genderless stick figures, heads tottering on withered bodies, wearing remnants of striped uniforms. Or worse, wearing nothing at all; standing against time, unprotected from weather, tedium, fear, pain. I saw people reduced to skulls with fierce eyes, skulls with dull eyes, skulls with no eyes.

Tears dripped down my face, dropped in warm splotches on my hands. I held myself sitting on the floor of my parents' room and sobbed for all those dead souls. I looked at every picture in the book again and again and again, driven by two wildly opposing impulses: moral outrage and morbid curiosity. Moral outrage gave me the courage to keep turning the pages. But morbid curiosity provided the unremitting interest. I poured over every gruesome detail of every gritty image. Somewhere in the middle I entered into the images themselves. Suddenly, I *was* every dead child denied a future, every dead Jew denied a grave. It seemed that I myself stood for a moment at the precipice between life and death. I wanted to die so I would never have to witness this kind of pain again; never acknowledge its possibility. Then I thought that I should live but cry for the rest of my life. Next I thought that God had died and I would stop living. Finally, the sobs subsided. I knew I was alive and that I would laugh again. And I decided that God had not died because in 1964 a child was kneeling on the carpeted floor of her parents' comfortably decorated bedroom, forcing herself to confront someone else's evil, her own shame and crying. Part of my idea of God had died. My innocence had departed, but God was still around somewhere.

The images of Auschwitz lodged so deeply into my psyche that they threatened to become my own memories and I struggled to put them away. The distractions of my own fully-lived adolescence helped, but willed forgetting was more important. I knew that I could not live my life in the shadow of the Holocaust. I talked myself out of it the way a small child will talk herself out of a recurring nighttime fear. I was already beginning to reject the Holocaust as a cornerstone of my personal identity when I had that conversation with my mother in the car. Her answer jarred me, making me wonder if I was wrong. It took me decades to finally figure out an answer I could live with.

My sense of being Jewish continued to be embodied in the rhythm of my days and seasons. Friday meant Shabbat dinner. Sunday meant going to Sunday school. Fall meant the High Holy Days. Winter meant Chanukah and Spring meant Passover. I don't think I would have progressed much beyond this circadian sense of Judaism had it not been for a Bible study group my mother organized when I was in fifth grade. It grew out of an adult study group she and my father belonged to. Three other couples in the group had daughters around my age who seemed to love learning as much as I did. Concerned about our Jewish education, our parents arranged for us to meet for two hours in one another's homes every Thursday afternoon for a year and a half. Our teacher, Mr. Morss, who was also the lower school principal at Park, assigned us passages to read during the week and we gradually worked our way through Genesis, Exodus and parts of the three remaining books.

Mr. Morss had high expectations for both the quality and the quantity of our participation. "I don't know" was an unacceptable answer to his questions. On these afternoons, a different Judaism began to emerge for me. I began to understand that it was more than a series of holidays and optional practices—it was a history of a people, *my* people. While others skimmed the pages of "begats" and found them boring, I found them mesmerizing. "These are the descendants of Shem: Shem was one hundred years old when he begot Arpachshad, two years after the Flood. . . . And Arpachshad lived four hundred three years after begetting Shelah; and he begot sons and daughters. Shelah had lived thirty years when he begot Eber. . . . When Nahor had lived twenty-nine years, he begot Terah. . . . When Terah had lived seventy years, he begot Abram, Nahor and Haran. . . and Haran begot Lot. . . . And Abram and Nahor took themselves wives; the name of Abram's wife was Sarai. . . ." The sound of those exotic, ancient names transfixed me with the notion that if laid out in a line they could form an almost endless chain that led directly from Adam and Eve to me. Sometimes at night, as I read the assigned passages, I would visualize God clicking beads on a celestial abacus as He counted the number of Jews. We were his great math problem—how to make a few into many.

I began to experiment with expressions of piety. I felt so noble and pure climbing into my bed each night to read the Bible. I thought piety was something I could slip on over my soul the same way I slipped a nightgown on over my head. I felt certain God would notice. "Look, there is that thoughtful, young girl wrestling with My words and trying to make sense of them. Isn't she a brave, exceptional little soul!" I *hoped* God would notice. Until the night I was

feeling especially pure and primed to receive the words of God and
opened my Bible to the biggest brown spider I had ever seen. With
a scream, I leapt from the bed and hurled the book against the wall,
all thoughts of sanctity and sacred texts instantly abandoned. Sheep-
ishly, I crept across the room to retrieve the book and found one
mashed spider, one page of Genesis blackened with spider guts, and
the beginnings of true humility. An authentic pietist would *never*
have lost it so easily. One creepy spider and holiness got the heave-
ho! Trepidation replaced righteousness in my nighttime readings
from that moment on. I didn't stop reading the wonderful words but
I stopped congratulating myself for it and acquired a new caution.
Anything that could be put on that easily could be taken off just as
easily. Piety wasn't something I could simply put on. It had to come
from someplace deep inside. A place I had not yet learned to locate.

I also began to puzzle over this God of the Old Testament who
wasn't anything like the kindly grandfather version that permeated
American culture. This God was *tough*. He tested Abraham and
pushed him right to the brink just to measure his faith. And I thought
my teachers and parents had high expectations! This God let Moses
get all the way to the Promised Land and then said, "Sorry, you broke
one of My important rules. I can't let you cross over. I don't change
My rules for anyone. If I started doing that no one would take Me seriously. And what I have to say is too important not to be taken
seriously."

This God meant business. He scared me a little because He didn't
leave much margin for error. This God sent spiders to crawl out of
the Bibles of little girls who were starting to be too pleased with
themselves for all the wrong reasons. It wasn't easy to be a Jew with
this kind of God, but it seemed like an interesting challenge. It felt
like something worth taking on.

"Grandpa" Moses

The business of growing up, however, soon proved more urgent.
Questions of theology and religious identity receded into the background as Judaism became the incidental backdrop for the more

pressing drama of adolescence. The way I had been taught to practice Judaism was of little use other than as a handy seasonal divider
and an admirable intellectual standard: Jews were smart. Jews asked
good questions. They liked to think. They reflected, then they acted.
These notions complemented my school's educational philosophy.
Park School was organized around the principle that effective learning occurred when students took personal responsibility for their
learning. Only as a student did my sense of myself as a Jew stay in
the foreground. Athletic and socially active, I remained deeply committed to my classroom work. I loved learning of all kinds and while
I did not know that we were the people of the book, I knew we
were a people who believed in the power of books and the liberation that learning enabled. I knew that Judaism revered the intellect
and considered learning a holy activity. Sometimes I felt that learning was holy, too.

Increasingly, however, I believed that the best and most authentic expression of Judaism was through philanthropy. My grandfather, Joseph Meyerhoff, now held major positions in national and
international Jewish organizations. He was often lauded as an exem-
plary leader, a modest and generous man. When my sixth grade Sunday school teacher gave us the assignment of profiling an important
Jew, I chose my grandfather. The rest of the class handed in projects
featuring various dead people—Moses, Abraham, Henrietta Szold or
Theodore Herzl—yet I got to do one on my own living flesh and
blood! Grandpa was far more real and much more important to me
than Moses.

We attended several banquets that featured him as the honoree,
and I began getting used to the idea that Judaism, philanthropy and
our name were synonymous. It was exciting to see my surname in
news stories and at public events. From a modest beginning as a
builder of single-family homes, my grandfather, with the help of his
son-in-law and my father, had grown the business into a commercial
and residential real estate enterprise that had instant local name
recognition. I liked the feeling of being part of an important family
although I wasn't always sure how much of the recognition we
enjoyed had to do with my family's communal leadership and

generosity and how much had to do with the real estate we developed. For my parents and grandparents, it wasn't even a question. Leadership, philanthropy and business success were inextricably linked. Over and over, I heard them make the same observation: "Money brings great privileges, chief among them the pleasure of giving it away."

I liked this honest, straightforward axiom. It seemed a simple truth that could illuminate the challenge of living a meaningful life when blessed with many privileges. It gave me and my siblings an immutable sense of personal responsibility to be charitable, a belief that this responsibility was not only innately Jewish but specifically *ours*.

Like most kids, I watched what my elders did more than listened to what they said. And to their credit, they spent more time doing than talking about philanthropy. Significantly, they acted more like philanthropy was an obligation than a choice—as if it were something they would do even if it *didn't* bring them pleasure. This particular lesson took completely.

But other lessons failed. I had no reverence for worship even though I had been taught in confirmation class that worship was an important part of being a Jew. The more important lesson was the one my parents were teaching me. We lived in an anti-religious household, one in which organized Jewish worship was scorned and other alternatives—home-grown services and serious study—were only superficially or sporadically embraced. My parents' resistance to organized religion was powerful, deeply felt and deliberately transmitted.

Looking back, I can theorize on reasons for their resistance, but far more important than my retroactive speculation is the fact that, at the time, I received their biases uncritically. I had no sense—and no reason to believe—that Judaism was a whole way of life. It was an essential part of my past, but of no immediate use in shaping my present. So I left it by the side of the road: A beat-up, serviceable piece of luggage I no longer had sufficient commitment to lug around. I didn't care about learning Hebrew while I could immerse myself in French, the language of diplomacy. I didn't want to know about

Israel while trying to master the intricacies of the history of *my* native country—the United States of America. I had no need for synagogue when my life was so full of school. The few times I did attend synagogue as a teenager I struggled to bring a full intent to the act of prayer. How confused I was to discover that most people prayed to get through it, not to be in it! What did Judaism care about the trauma of female development other than to cite women as future reproductive vessels? Confirmation class was merely a place to meet boys. The one meaningful session that entire year occurred when a teacher attempted to analyze Simon and Garfunkel's "Bridge over Troubled Waters" as an expression of Jewish values. It was a tortured effort, but at least he was trying to intrude Judaism into our world rather than intrude into our world and force us to deal with Judaism.

Looking at Judaism through Stained Glass Windows

Around this same time, I visited several churches from various Christian denominations. Until then I had been in only one church, a small, rural stone structure where our "mother's helper," Chris, got married. My mother wept copiously (not solely for joy), and my little sister and I served as the flower girls. From a distance, the church looked like something out of a fairy tale with its graceful stone steeple poking up to the blue sky and bright green grass creeping straight to the cobbled walls that surrounded it. Inside, one stained glass window threw an entrancing splash of color across the burnished flagstone floor. The chapel was remarkably cool for a steamy August day in Baltimore. But as soon as the ceremony began, I had to concentrate on two things: not giggling at my best friend, Soupy, who was making faces at me from her pew seat; and not scratching my hand, still swollen from a bee sting that had nearly killed me a few weeks before. I didn't pay any more attention to the space because I was focusing all my attention on not scratching and not laughing.

I next entered a church during our Sunday school visitation program. This time, it got my full and immediate attention. As I stepped out of the vestibule and into the magnificent leaping space of the cathedral itself, my breath swept from my lungs and soared skyward to skim the vaulting ceilings painted, tiled and bedecked with story. Wherever I turned, some other gorgeous sight sucked the air from me, left me slightly gaspy and lightheaded as if I had accidentally stumbled upon some exotic high-altitude principality. "Why," I thought, "couldn't synagogues be *this* beautiful?" Why were all the sanctuaries I knew so utilitarian, so uninspiring, so multi-purpose-like, as if the architects were designing a town hall with a few holy objects thrown in for good measure? If religion was supposed to beautify our lives, why were our sanctuaries so uniformly pedestrian and unimaginative? Even as I thought about the differences, I registered the effect of these gorgeous spaces. I loved them! They made some sleepy part of me come wide awake, pounding at the inside of my chest to be let out. They made me want to *think* about God. The nooks and crannies of the churches we visited fascinated me. Our architecture held no surprises, no hidden places to kneel, reflect or pray. Whatever you did in synagogue was in full view of anyone who cared to watch in the wide open spaces of our sanctuaries. But churches gave you spaces for private moments. I wondered if the Christian sins I'd heard and read about required separate, secret spaces to contain them.

Although the churches inspired me with their beauty, the visits also reinforced my earlier childhood view of Jesus. It continued to strike me as odd that a religion would glorify a man who was hurt and continually dying in full view of his worshiping public. It seemed to me that religion ought to help us live our lives, not prepare us for our deaths. At thirteen, I did not understand that the two are directly connected. I could not fathom the idea of someone else dying for *my* sins. The whole idea seemed so unfair! Why should someone else have to suffer because of what I did—even if it was in advance, *especially* if it was in advance? I had trouble even with the Christian notion of sins.

As I understood it, Christianity suggested that we were all bound to commit them. If we were *bound* to be sinful, I wondered, then why bother not to be? Perhaps, I reasoned, trying not to is what made us better people, but Judaism had already taught me that if I did break one of God's rules I would be responsible for it. The idea of the Catholic confession was particularly strange to me. It seemed to grant priests unfair power over their congregants' lives. In some way that I couldn't pinpoint, the transaction appeared unethical. I could not imagine a rabbi imposing penance for anything. I also found it perplexing to think of Jesus as the Messiah. First of all, God wasn't supposed to take human form in that way and second, I didn't think we were supposed to take the idea of the Messiah literally. It seemed to me to be one of God's great allegorical allusions. It was the *idea* of the Messiah we were supposed to embrace, not the actual coming itself. Once we got there, what then? And if Jesus was the Messiah and he had already come, then why were things still such a mess?

Finally, although I loved the magnificent spaces in which Christianity housed its faith, I was troubled by the profusion of what I could only characterize as idols. Jesus was the central one around which all the others revolved. The Madonna especially confounded me. I had studied basic biology. The Virgin Birth was another one of those allegorical ideas. It couldn't actually be taken *seriously*. But the multiple sentimental images of Mary in almost every Christian sanctuary we visited affirmed that indeed it was taken *very* seriously. I saw renderings of the Last Supper, saints preserved in stained glass, Madonna alone, Madonna with child, Madonna with dying adult son, John the Baptist before and after, and always, everywhere, the crucifixion figure. I became quite a connoisseur of that icon. In a macabre takeoff on "Queen for a Day," I ran a silent applause meter in my head, rating the various depictions for composition, accuracy, bloodiness and persuasiveness. It seemed to me that Jews preserved their history in text which we read during worship. Christians captured their history in images with which they surrounded themselves during worship.

I never stopped to think how odd it was that my clearest and most penetrating understanding of my own religious tradition was achieved only by contrasting it to *another* religious tradition. I knew more about who I was by declaring who I was *not* than by spontaneously defining the major precepts of Judaism. I had neither the vocabulary, the context nor the confidence to do that properly.

The G-Word

When I entered Duke University in the fall of 1970, at age seventeen, I was one of five hundred undergraduate Jews. Within days of arriving, I followed a piece of advice from each of my parents. At the urging of my mother, I went to a Hillel meeting, albeit with apprehensive visions of Jews conspicuously, maybe even belligerently, celebrating their Judaism. I was certain they would try to coerce me into joining an embarrassing group activity like the hora dances I had refused to participate in during the years I attended *bar* and *bat mitzvah* parties. By and large, they were a strange group of young men and women from whom I felt almost instantly alienated save for one pipe-smoking, wickedly funny junior. I never went back to Hillel, but he followed me straight out of that first meeting to become my first college boyfriend and a lifelong friend.

My father had suggested that I take a course in basic world religions. I didn't think I would like a survey course, but his advice sent me to the religion department listings. I chose Theology 101, mostly because the names in the syllabus sounded exotic: Kierkegaard, Niebuhr, Schopenhauer, Tillich, Buber, Frankl. I wondered if their ideas could be as interesting as their names. I wondered if I might be able to think about the same things that they had.

That course transformed me, revealing an intellectual rigor I did not know I possessed as I struggled to master a new lexicon of words and concepts: telos, ethos, firmament of standards, ontology, phenomenology, tautology, revelation, secularization, covenant. I had registered on a whim, anticipating an intellectual flirtation. Instead I found myself immersed in a full-blown romance, thoroughly enchanted by the sound, texture and nuances of my new academic love. As I learned more, I realized there was a missing link in my concept of Judaism as a religion. I needed it to be more than a history of a people, a string of holidays punctuated by family meals, an ancient prescription for law and order. I needed to better understand the

8/31/18

source of its power and its vitality. Theology revealed the questions I needed but had not known enough to ask. My limited Jewish knowledge prevented me from coming up with any of the answers, but I knew I needed to figure out how God really worked in my tradition.

Prior to that, I could not remember ever having a serious, sustained discussion about God with *anyone:* parents, teachers, friends or siblings. The only sustained discussion I could recall wasn't *about* God, but *with* God when the "We will bury you" ads, featuring a stone-faced Khrushchev, aired during a cold war awareness shock campaign. I'm not sure who the intended TV audience was, but I presented a particularly susceptible and vulnerable ten-year-old target. Every time I saw or heard one of the ads, my stomach contracted and I registered the shocking imminence of my own mortality. I truly believed this man could bury me and everyone and everything I cared about in the world with no more remorse than I might feel if I accidentally ran over an ant with my bike. His flat, inscrutable expression terrified me, and his straightforward statement sounded more like a prophecy than a threat. Compounding my fear was my parents' absolute refusal to join the bomb-shelter building frenzy, calmly stating that if it came to nuclear war they didn't want to survive. "What about me?" I wanted to cry out. "*I* want to survive!" But I kept silent, knowing on a rational level that they were right and not wanting to appear childish, selfish or weak in their eyes. Instead, I talked to God. This wasn't a typical kid-cutting-a-deal-with-the-deity conversation: "God, if you will do this *one thing* I promise never to be bad again." It was a sober, reasoned exchange. "God," I wanted to know, "why can't you get President Kennedy and Khrushchev to talk to each other? I'm sure that if you could just get them in a room together that they could work all of this out. They really need to be by themselves where nobody else is watching so they don't have to worry about what other people are thinking of them. It's not good for little children to be scared to go to sleep every night because they think that the atom bomb is going to drop on their house! Please, God, I'm sure they don't actually want to kill little kids—adults maybe, but not all the children! Now, here's how I think you should handle it. . . ."

These discussions (they *were* discussions because I was certain God was listening to me and responding even though I couldn't hear the response) reached their peak with the Cuban missile crisis in 1962 when I spoke to God sometimes four or five times a day. God, I assumed, was the only being with more authority than the President of the United States and the Premier of Russia. I did not fancy that my personal intercession was responsible when the crisis was successfully resolved, but I stopped communing with God. With my greatest fear eliminated, I couldn't imagine bothering God with my tiny, everyday concerns. The God I believed in was not a personal God. This God was only interested in the global big stuff. And I never heard talk of God in my household or my Sunday school. God wasn't essential to my definition of myself as a Jew, a realization that highlights the essential ambiguity of the religious identity I was bequeathed: I was certain of my religious affiliation yet devoid of grounded religious belief and understanding. I was convinced that I was Jewish, yet confused about what that meant in terms of God.

So in search of the Jewish God I did not know, I took a course called "The Old Testament" taught by Eric Meyers, head of the newly established Jewish Studies program. A tall, handsome Jewish man with a blinding white smile that he flashed on and off with the frequency and unpredictability of a firefly, Eric's true love was biblical archaeology. After archaeology, I think what Eric loved most was making the Bible come alive for cynical, often disinterested students. As a young professor attuned to our baby boomer sensibilities, he understood we would never take the words in the Bible at face value. But as a biblical scholar, he insisted we understand that we were dealing with a historical document that recorded events, myths and concepts. Their reality was immaterial; our main concern was their context. We couldn't begin to understand the meaning until we understood the history, politics, economics and geography that framed them. If we really wanted to understand the Pentateuch (the Five Books of Moses) and what it meant, we had to understand who created it; to know that this was the progressive story of an entire people who were struggling to achieve maturity. Their regular testing of the limits of covenant required corrective responses, patience, punishment. Even YHWH (as budding would-be biblical scholars, we were taught to use the tetragrammaton for God's name) developed, transforming from angry, vengeful autocrat to thoughtful, compassionate teacher. Finally, we had to understand that, for a primitive people, monotheism was an astonishing intellectual and spiritual achievement. It was enough to make you believe in God.

Finding Myself in the Ashes

After a summer on Duke's archaeological dig in Israel, I declared my major in religion. I didn't think about it seriously as a career. I just loved it. I signed up for a course entitled "God After Auschwitz," determined that I would have a purely intellectual engagement with the material. I didn't have time or space in my life for histrionic identification with the "core" Jewish experience of the Holocaust. I had already done that when I was twelve and rejected it as dangerous and flawed.

I almost succeeded. I studied Richard Rubinstein, Victor Frankl, Hannah Arendt and Elie Wiesel, but could not embrace their despair or their desperate expressions of hope. The Holocaust had nothing to do with me: it could not inform my worldview. I set up an emotional wall to prevent it from challenging my fundamental optimism about humanity or my sense of security as an American Jew. Professor Meyers challenged me regularly as I stood my ground.

"How can you say this had nothing to do with you? These were your people! They are a part of your history."

"They were not *my* people. They were mostly poor, superstitious peasants. They wore strange clothes, raised chickens and lived in huts."

"They were doctors, lawyers, writers, professors, concert violinists, businessmen, mothers, husbands, fathers, wives. They were Jewish families. *Whole* families wiped out. They could have been your family."

"They could have been," I countered with a shrug of my shoulders, "but they weren't."

My defenses collapsed one night as we watched newsreels that told the shameful story of the *St. Louis,* a refugee ship that returned to Europe after being turned away at every port she went to in the Western Hemisphere. Nearly every passenger subsequently died in the Holocaust. From the midst of those flickering images a child's face suddenly soared up at me from the screen. I looked into her eyes and knew I could no longer deny my connection to her. She was my sister, my cousin, my aunt, my friend, my self. She was gone—and I had to take her place, to bear witness, to make her history live. Tears began to leak from my eyes. Soon I had to leave. Dr. Meyers followed me out as I left and had the good sense to say nothing but to simply hold me for a moment. His touch was very important at that instant. It made me feel not quite so alone with my new knowledge. I returned to my dorm room and, between rounds of crying, I wrote a letter to my parents that laid claim to my heritage and my history. For the first time, I took responsibility for the central lesson of Judaism: Jews forge community through time. If I truly opted for Judaism, I could not pick and choose the points on the timeline that pleased me or skip past the ones that frightened, alienated or embarrassed me.

But there was a darker, less obvious explanation for my resistance. Until that evening, I did not want to acknowledge how much I had invested in my non-Semitic looks: hazel eyes, light brown straight hair, high cheekbones, small nose and athletic build. People were usually surprised to discover I was Jewish and I always delighted in the trick. "Passing," I suddenly understood, had crept insidiously into my definition of what it meant to be an American Jew. Passing kept me safe and allowed me to participate in American life without challenge. Passing was my *passport.* It let me be an American on American terms but a Jew on my own terms. If I passed, no one would have to know that although I looked and acted like any other comfortable, white American kid, I was only two generations and a steerage boat ride away from my Russian peasant background. If I passed, no one would have to know I was a Jew unless I chose to let them know. If I passed, I could be the master of my own destiny. The Holocaust blew away that convenient deceit. It was shameful, cowardly and, I finally had to admit, hopeless to trade on genetic accident to my advantage. I dropped the option on that advantage that evening. From that moment on, I took pains to identify myself as a Jew lest anyone jump to conclusions based on my appearance alone. It was suddenly important that people who didn't know me knew that about me *first*. If they wanted to know me afterward, it was their choice—but it would be a conscious choice. I could no longer deny that little girl, the German doctor, the Czech concert violinist, the Polish Chasid, the Russian chicken farmer. I could not deny them and remain a Jew who loved herself.

As it turns out, Mom was right. But so was I. Every Jew born after the Holocaust has to confront that event as part of their heritage, as one of the prisms through which they receive and develop their Jewish identity. As the political culmination of 2,000 years of church-directed anti-Semitic polemic and action, it proved in the starkest way imaginable how alone the Jew is in a non-Jewish world. It confirmed what centuries of cruel Diaspora experience have ground into our collective Jewish conscience: even when we don't see ourselves as "other," others will.

Interpreted solely in this way, however, the legacy of the Holocaust breeds caution and mistrust at best, paranoia and hatred at worst. It fell to my generation, the first generation of Jews born "innocent" of this event, to begin to work out how future generations might come to live with it.

Mom was right, and I couldn't ignore that. I had to allow the Holocaust to influence my Jewish identity. Judaism is nothing without its memories. If every religion has a primary refrain, then ours is "remember." Ashes, exile and torture are part of my Jewish inheritance, one strand on the DNA of my Jewish peoplehood gene.

Decades later, I now understand why I was right to resist that triad being the *centerpiece* of my Jewish identity. Revenge is a powerful motivator for the avenger—less so for his children. If I accepted the Holocaust as my starting point, where could I go from there? Especially if I lived in comfort and safety with the possibility of real religious freedom—a true American in the latter half of the twentieth century. The Holocaust/Israel story had genuine religious meaning for my parents. They were acting as agents of redemption. There is no more powerful religious work than the work of redemption. But they didn't teach me the meaning of their example *within a religious context*. And because they couldn't place it in one, neither could I. They asked me to accept their *particular* history and not *our* exceptional history. They connected me to the isolated historical event, not to the ongoing narrative of our people. Disconnected from our story as a people, detached from the Jewish pursuit of a sacred destiny in partnership with God, the Holocaust and my parents' response to it failed to instruct me on how to live my life. As an isolated event, the only lessons it taught were political ones. Yet even at twelve, I understood that a meaningful life cannot be constructed on the altar of politics.

To Be or Not to Be . . . an American or a Jew?

My home-based Jewish recollections are often warm and surrounded by good intention. But they contain minimal religious observance since my parents saw religious ritual as a means to an end—never the end in itself. Viewed that way, religious ritual was never more than a utilitarian nuisance, something best dispensed with quickly. In our post-Enlightenment era, strict ritual observance was for the people who lacked the good sense to value and guard their own autonomy. But people who revere personal autonomy are just putting faith in people above faith in God. They forget that absolute autonomy is a myth in either case. Ritual observance *does* impose limits on autonomy. That's the point of it: to suggest that autonomy itself is an illusion. Anyone who has conceded their mortality instantly recognizes that truth. Ritual reminds us regularly—directly and symbolically—that it's God who really calls all the shots. And accepting the "yoke" of God's authority was the feature of religion my parents most actively resisted. They didn't like it at home and they didn't like it in community.

To be sure, my parents—especially my mother—recognized the transformative power of ritual. She consciously and regularly introduced new traditions and practices into our lives. The ritual dimension of our family life was complex and rich, but it wasn't linked to any preexisting system that had greater authority than my parents.

Only in our annual *seder* did our need to create our own rituals intersect directly with Jewish tradition. I don't know which was more compelling: the ritual we were inventing or the one we were reenacting. Maybe it was the combination itself, the fact that as a family we were working out together how to make this central Jewish drama our own. Maybe the intoxicating Jewish energy I reveled in each year was the charged air of religious authenticity. Following a form for recalling our historic liberation freed us to liberate ourselves. Apart from lighting the Shabbat candles and hearing my father recite a Shabbat prayer of his own invention, our first night family *seder* is my single most powerful Jewish memory from childhood.

Not surprisingly, I carried most of the Jewish lessons I learned from my parents directly into my life as a young wife and mother. It was a given that I would marry a Jew. Nonnegotiable, as far as I was concerned. But I didn't intend to meet my future husband on a blind date during winter break of my senior year in college, nor did I intend to fall in love with Nelson the night we met or decide that we would marry only a few days later. Nelson and I knew that we wanted children and agreed that I would stay home with our children while they were young. So I knew I would not pursue the career in drama I had been contemplating because I believed families and theatrical careers were incompatible.

The nine months of our engagement raced by. I remember a lot of laughter, but not a single conversation about the quality of the Jewish life we would share or the kind of Jewish home we would create. Instead, we discussed paint colors, furniture choices, career opportunities and wedding guests.

Nelson and I were married in a private ceremony at my parents' home. Dr. Louis L. Kaplan officiated. The former president of the Baltimore Hebrew College, Lou was the executive director of the Joseph Meyerhoff Fund, which had been founded by my grandfather. A learned man and brilliant teacher—beloved by our family for his radical views and pragmatic approach to Judaism—Lou consistently denounced most Jewish ritual as nonsense and nine-tenths of Jewish prayer as ridiculous. Lou met with us for an hour before he agreed to marry us. I don't remember much of what transpired except that he called me "darling" frequently and posed us a riddle about two chimney sweeps. I do remember the wedding as intimate, beautiful and joyous.

Within eighteen months, Nelson and I had our first child, a son whom we named Sam. At Nelson's insistence, Sam was circumcised while still in the hospital. We held a ceremonial *bris* in our home eight days after his birth. Dr. Kaplan officiated. A few weeks later, Lou asked me when we were having Sam's *Pidyon Haben.* "His pidyon what?" I asked.

Lou described an arcane ritual that acknowledged God's claim on the first-born Jewish son. Like the first fruits and the first animal offspring that we were obligated to sacrifice, we were supposed to give our first-born male child to God. Of course, we Jews had done away with human sacrifice long ago, so a financial transaction had been created to substitute for the sacrifice.

"Say that again, Lou," I said. "We give you the money. Then we give you the kid. Then we buy him back from you? What *for?*" Even after he explained that it's a way of acknowledging that everything we have is on loan from God, I still didn't understand it. I simply had no context for making sense of symbolic religious ritual.

"We'll do it if you say we have to, Lou. But I still don't get it."

"Most people don't, darling, but you do have to do it. It's important." I didn't hesitate when Lou said we had to do something Jewish. I trusted him to keep us on the straight and narrow even if I didn't know exactly where the path was going.

We held that ceremony at Nelson's parents' home. When Alex was born eighteen months later, we marked his *bris* at home using *The Jewish Catalogue* for inspiration. Dr. Kaplan was unavailable so we created our own ceremony. And when Lindsay was born four years later, we held a naming ceremony officiated by Lou, on my sister's porch. When Josepha arrived four years after Lindsay, we invited friends and relatives to celebrate with us in our home. Lou conferred her Hebrew name upon her while I conducted a ceremony that included all three of her siblings. It never occurred to me or Nelson that our synagogue might be the appropriate setting for a baby-naming ceremony. That is how disconnected we were from any sense of belonging to a congregational community. In fact, when my mother died in 1988 and the two rabbis from Chizuk Amuno Congregation came to pay a *shiva* call at my father's house, I was surprised to see them. I was so ignorant of the role of the pulpit rabbi in congregants' lives that I did not realize this was one of their standard responsibilities. Instead I was secretly touched that they had taken time out of their busy schedules to come. The first Jewish family ritual that we ever celebrated in synagogue took place a year after my mother's death and fourteen and a half years after our wedding. It was our son Sam's *bar mitzvah.*

Up to age forty, I was aware of being Jewish, but I didn't have a comprehensive view of Judaism that allowed me to integrate it into my daily life. I defined myself as a Jew mostly in counterpoint to what I understood to be the prevailing principles of Christianity. I saw Judaism through the lens of my Jewish notion of Christianity. This meant that all of my Jewish understanding had to pass through that filter first—producing major distortions and misunderstandings. The problem was further compounded by contrasting a religious tradition that was strictly religious with a religious tradition that had been reduced to a civil and ethnic distillate. Coming from the second model, the comparison only bred contempt instead of the profound respect I ought to have had for another's sacred beliefs.

No lasting convictions arose to suggest that my fundamental identity or my life choices could be primarily influenced by or permanently shaped by being a Jew. Nothing emerged to allow me to use Judaism as a bridge between myself and my community, to make the leap and achieve the connection to community that Hillel's teaching "Do not separate yourself from the community" commands us to seek. And of course, among the people I admired I had very few models of a Jewish life that might be lived in this fully integrated way. I grew up in a loving, orderly home that was rich in intellectual, political and physical activity but religiously—ritually and spiritually—deprived, deeply American but marginally Jewish, genuinely decent but barely observant.

All this registered with stunning ferocity during an early session of the women's Torah study group I belong to. We were discussing the nature of our identity as American Jews when our teacher, Rabbi Joel Zaiman, asked the disarmingly simple question, "If someone asked who you were, would you say an American or a Jew first?" My response was immediate but truthful—"an American." Right away, I was ashamed of my answer because I knew it was the "wrong" one and most of the class had instantly volunteered the "right" one. Shame was immediately compounded by anger at Rabbi Zaiman because the question itself was so unfair. It was the same tired accusation of competing loyalties that had plagued Diaspora Jews for centuries and resulted in persecution, death or eviction from communities in which they lived. Happily, the world in which we lived no longer required us to make such choices or statements. What a cheap shot! How dare he pull the old loyalty oath skeleton from the closet! How manipulative!

Vacillating between rage and shame, I suddenly realized how skillfully Rabbi Zaiman had demonstrated that while the rest of the world might not care about my answer anymore, *I* did. The point was that privately we make these choices all the time. At that moment, I was appalled that my family's history and success in this country had conditioned the "American" response in me. Not only was it the response I was ready to volunteer, it was the response I *believed* in. Today, four years later, my answer is "A Jew first, but now I want to learn how to be both at the same time."

3

How to Enter the Sanctuary the First Time You Don't Have an Excuse

Na'aseh v'nishmah: *"We shall do and we shall hear."*

—Exodus 24:7

The first week of March 1993 was a rough week. The kids, ages seven, eleven, fifteen and seventeen, needed more of my attention. My husband was consumed with his medical practice and my community work had become increasingly demanding. I was exhausted, irritable and confused about my life.

Since early fall, I'd been overseeing an initiative in Jewish education sponsored by the philanthropic fund my siblings and I ran. After months of planning and negotiating, the committee of rabbis and educators I chaired had settled on the topic for the first year: *tefillah,* or prayer. When the topic was first proposed at a meeting in early January, I thought people were talking about those funny little things men wrapped around their arms and stuck on their heads that make them look like unfortunate tourniquet victims with hematomas. I was still fairly blasé about my Jewish ignorance so I asked what they were talking about. As I listened and learned over the course of two meetings, I became conversant enough on *tefillah* to begin using a whole new vocabulary.

So I was well-prepared when I presented an update on the project to my siblings in mid-February, and especially eager to parade my newly acquired knowledge. It wasn't too different from the childhood excitement of wearing a new pair of shoes on the first day of school. I wanted to show off my shiny, just-out-of-the-box leather.

8/21/18

I announced that the program would focus on *tefillah,* the vehicle that "best enables Jews to gather together and proclaim their Jewishness in community!" These were good words, a reasonable approximation of one of the things *tefillah* can be about.

But siblings have an irritating knack for calling our bluff. "So, Lee-lee," my brother, Joe, said, "when's the last time you . . . um . . . gathered?"

He had me—and we all knew it. I laughed like a kid who's been caught in a game of tag and admitted that I'd last "gathered" during the High Holy Days. I hadn't enjoyed it, but at least I'd been there, "unlike some *other* people I knew."

The moment passed, but the aftershock stayed with me for days. I was a fraud. I'd known it all along. I just hadn't wanted to admit it because if I did that I just might have to *do* something about it. Along with most of the leaders in the Jewish community, I was wearing the crown of privilege without having earned the true right to claim it. I served on task forces, chaired committees, led strategic planning initiatives and contributed to a number of Jewish and non-Jewish causes. I'd done my time and paid my dues. I'd participated willingly, proudly and often self-importantly, but I was still a fraud. What did I really know about Judaism that I could confidently cite as the source for all this devotion and activity? What did I really know about Jewish *community* other than Federation board meetings, agency programs, campaign events, the Holocaust and Israel? What did I know about being a Jew other than how to serve on a board, read an agency budget projection, write a check to charity, light candles on Shabbat and attribute all these good deeds to my "Jewish" upbringing?

I knew that something huge was missing from the equation "Volunteer work + Contribution + Israel + Holocaust + nostalgia + 2 candles once a week = a Jew." I claimed that I was living a life based on convictions, and that the anchor for most of these convictions was Judaism. Yet, when I probed what I truly knew about Judaism, and examined how I lived my convictions *as a Jew,* I found neither substance or dependability. My anchor actually rested in sand. At any moment, I could slip my mooring and drift with no means of returning to safe harbor.

I sensed that the anchorage I sought might be synagogue, but I was loathe to admit it. It meant I'd actually have to *go there* to get it, and going to synagogue had about as much appeal to me as my husband's description gave baseball: "Hours of tedium punctuated by moments of excitement." Synagogue gave me the same grinding stomachache I used to get as a kid when my mother dragged me to symphony concerts because they were "good" for me. Synagogue was a potential dose of spiritual castor oil: It might be good for me eventually, but it sure would be tough getting it down. And yet, why had I been toying with the idea for months? Why had I dragged my kids a few years before to the first day services for Sukkot? What had I hoped to find there other than the raised eyebrows and wry smile of the rabbi, and the ritual director grabbing my wrist as he growled, "You can't touch the *lulavs*. They're for the people who reserved them in advance!"?

What did I think might reside in that cavernous, unfriendly place? A whisper careening across the centuries, passed by so swiftly that I almost missed it: "Community." In the other ear I heard: "Continuity." It was impossible to have one without the other and both were the current obsession of the Federation world.

I was beginning to question whether the Jewish community I knew had the power to sustain Judaism into the twenty-first century. Steep intermarriage rates, falling annual Federation campaigns and declining numbers of willing and able Jewish leaders gave me good reason to doubt our viability. Suspecting that some of the necessary sustenance might be found in synagogue, I realized I could no longer dismiss it if I didn't want to remain a fraud.

Finding a Place in *Shul*

One of the ironies of this story is that the synagogue we belong to, Chizuk Amuno Congregation, is "my husband's *shul*." Our children now represent the fifth generation of Hendler family membership. When Nelson and I married, it made no difference to me which *shul* we attended. I had a reflexive loyalty to Baltimore Hebrew Congregation because that's where my family had always belonged. But the *most* I could say about it was that I liked its sanctuary and I had a few warm fuzzy memories from the time I'd been there. All I remembered of Chizuk Amuno from my teenage visits there for the occasional *bar* or *bat mitzvah* was that I didn't like its sanctuary with its dark, mahogany details and awful electric ark—and I didn't understand the services. Since I knew I wouldn't be there very often, I reasoned, it didn't really matter whether I liked it or not. It felt good to make a concession to my husband so early in our marriage: "Of course we'll belong to Chizuk Amuno if it means that much to you."

So we joined and I dutifully trudged off to *shul* with him every Rosh Hashanah and Yom Kippur. As our four children arrived over a nine-and-a-half-year period, I experienced a surge of pride when we trotted them out for communal inspection each fall. I appreciated the admiring glances, the kind remarks. Still, it gave me a stomachache. The moment I walked into the sanctuary my stomach would start to churn. Every few minutes, I would check my watch and calculate how much longer we would have to stay. Occasionally, Nelson would announce he'd like to remain for the entire service. This was the equivalent of being told as a teenager that I'd been grounded for a week: stuck with absolutely no chance of a reprieve.

Unable to read Hebrew, I only read the English translations of a few prayers. If I felt particularly reflective on Yom Kippur, I made a *special* point of reading at least half of them: It seemed like an appropriate penance to be dutiful for some of the time I was there. Sometimes I leafed to the back of the *machzor,* the special High Holy Days prayer book, and wondered why we didn't use a few of the more contemporary reflections to relieve the sheer monotony of it all. On the rare occasion when I showed up for a *bar* or *bat mitzvah* ceremony, I might actually take out the *Chumash,* which has the entire cycle of Torah and Haftarah (selections from Prophets) readings and accompanying commentary, when it was time for the Torah service. I had an almost clinical response to the text; I admired its age and I was curious about its structure, but I didn't imagine it had much to say to me *personally.* I enjoyed hearing familiar tunes I recognized from my Reform upbringing, and I readily joined in. But most of the melodies were unfamiliar, and the *chazzan* (cantor) always seemed to be trying out a new tune to replace the traditional ones I knew. This left me confused and disoriented—always lagging a phrase or two behind everyone else.

I had to admit that there *was* something rather majestic in the spectacle of 1,800 human beings rising as one and reciting a prayer together on Rosh Hashanah. The *shofar* was a wonderful theatrical touch and its haunting call momentarily displaced my discomfort about being there. But basically, I didn't *get it.* The form and purpose of the services eluded me. I decided that they were for those unfortunate souls misguided enough to momentarily suspend critical thought, to blindly choose faith over reason. The only feature that ever made the service even remotely worthwhile was the sermon. I listened attentively to the rabbi's words, admired his skill, his style of weaving together contemporary and traditional texts, his intellectual rigor, his determination not to dumb his messages down. I remembered some sermons for days afterward. But even the prospect of a good sermon couldn't counteract the unavoidable tedium surrounding it. It wasn't enough to get me there on even a semi-regular basis.

So with major misgivings, I marched myself into *shul* on a Shabbat morning in March of 1993. It was my first faith gesture; it went against every lesson I had been taught about the nature and value of worship. I felt vulnerable, ignorant, naked before the eyes of a congregation from whose gaze I could not hide. I imagined that everyone was whispering about me, and I was certain of it when I heard one woman whisper, "That's the Meyerhoff girl. She married a Hendler. I wonder what *she's* doing here?" I clenched my jaw and chose the first free seat I could find in the back, so I would not have to bear up under the scrutiny of too many watchful eyes.

Today I could plot out my advancing comfort in synagogue on an expedition-style map that charts my progression toward the front of the sanctuary. I started out that first day in the far back on the right, moved gradually to the middle back on the left, then to the solid middle of the left side, and today sit in the front left section, five rows back from the *bimah,* the raised platform that holds the ark, the pulpits, and the reading table, and where most of the service is conducted. Now I understand the tiny, wizened lady with the little pink ribbon perched in her hair. I was in my phase of exploring the middle terrain of the sanctuary when she tapped me on the shoulder one morning and gripped my arm with her surprisingly strong hand.

"Honey, you're in *my* seat!" she whispered in obvious distress.

The irreverent part of me wanted to say, "*What?* Is your *name* on it?"

Fortunately, the part of me that respects my elders prevailed. Instead I said, "I'm so sorry. I didn't mean to. Please take it." I am now so miffed when someone parks themselves in *my* seat that I often rush to get to *shul* early on Saturday so this doesn't happen. If I'm late, I feel like the baby bear in "Goldilocks," anxious upon returning to the cottage, sensing that something must be awry and then dismayed almost beyond words if someone has indeed sat in *my* chair.

That was my first new lesson in community. Like a student in a classroom, *I* had a place in it and a physical location I could claim because other members of the community acknowledged my right to it. In turn, the community organized itself by holding certain expectations of its members: we had to *be* there. I knew immediately when someone wasn't and I worried about them: Were they ill? Was there a problem in their family? I made a mental note of their absence and it registered in a different way because the community was not whole without them. *I* was not as whole without them.

The act of collective worship—which I was beginning to understand after a few months of steady attendance—celebrated the individual even as it subsumed him or her. We couldn't worship as a group without the individuals, but the point of coming as individuals to the group was to submit our individual identity to our group identity: to admit that my humanity was identical to the person standing next to me and fourteen rows behind me and ten centuries before me. I knew that each of us stood puny before God, but that all of us stood *together* as *a people* capable of attaining holiness. We *needed* one another to achieve it. It was the first palpable evidence I had of the constant, elastic tension in Judaism between the individual and community. The air fairly sung with it when I was focused and open to its possibility.

Pride and Prejudice

To suggest that I knew this from my first voluntary foray into syna-gogue would give me far too much credit. But I got enough of a hint of it that first time to decide to return—even though returning was hard work. At the moment that I decided to walk into my sanctuary without the provisional excuse of High Holy Days or a *bar* or *bat mitzvah,* I was incredibly vulnerable, and my resolve was extremely tenuous. The most gentle wisecrack, the most subtle sidelong glance, the most sincere but thoughtless request—"Needed to get away from the kids?," "Did somebody die?," even "Would you like to dress the Torah?"—were nearly enough to send me scurrying for an exit, certain that this was not the place for me, never was and never would be.

My tremendous vulnerability came from a complicated mixture of ignorance, self-consciousness and pride. I was a third-generation American Jew. My family history epitomized the American Success Story. My paternal grandfather came to this country in 1906 at age six, from the Russian town of Pereschepina with his brothers, sis-ters, parents and entire life savings—$600. The business he built and ultimately sold made him a fortune. I considered myself incredibly lucky, worldly, well-educated, accomplished, culturally and socially adept. I served on the boards of many organizations and helped them raise money or undertake strategic planning. I had four healthy, thriving children and I'd been married to the same man for nineteen years. My life was comfortable, safe and rewarding. It would have been so easy to ignore my Jewish illiteracy and simply continue to do what I knew how to do.

Acknowledging my ignorance took honesty. Doing something about it required admitting that I was not nearly as powerful, com-petent and at home in the world as I thought I was—or as I wanted everyone else to believe I was. It also put me on a collision course with my pride. I realized that a significant part of my reluctance to give myself up to the Shabbat service was fear of submission, and that the earliest lessons I'd had in submission were closer to lessons in humiliation—not submitting to the kindness of a higher authority, but to the potential brutality and oppressiveness of it. My mother's unpredictable, often angry responses to weakness, mistakes or vulnerability taught me early on that submitting to authority was a risky business. My father's insistence on perfection sometimes made "trying" too trying to attempt. But I wasn't a child any more. It was time to let go of the years of conditioning—and time to stop acting like a child.

The next hurdle was learning how to maintain a sense of self while joining community. I so profoundly resisted the idea of being *in* Jewish community, yet I knew that I needed to drop this resistance to truly *be* a Jew. Doing this meant uprooting all the biases my parents had transmitted. They disapproved of synagogue (we belonged, but never went), Jewish neighborhoods (we didn't live in one), Jewish resorts (we went skiing in Maine, Colorado or Switzerland during our school vacations), Jewish country clubs (we had a family membership at one, but Mom and Dad just dropped us off there), Jewish expressions (we were not allowed to say *"Oy vay"* and I never heard the words *"Bubbe"* and *"Zayde"* until I was an adult), and Jewish national anthems (my mother forbade singing *"Hatikva"* at the end of the *seder,* stating emphatically that we were Americans, *not Israelis*). They even, at some level, disapproved of Jewish organizational life (both Mom and Dad dropped out of it in their mid-forties, fed up with much of what they encountered there, although this did not affect their financial giving nor their *active* encouragement of *our* involvement as young adults). The subliminal message I received was "Beware of Jews in large groups." Even more subversive was the suggestion that associating with Jews in these kinds of settings or adopting their clannish behaviors might prevent successful assimilation and real achievement. Being "too Jewish" was incompatible with being a true American.

It would have been easier for me to ferret out these messages if my parents had *said* these things to me. But they never did. Not given to introspection and analysis, they lived their lives by example in every respect. They simply made their choices and left the interpretation to us.

Mistakenly, I expected to come to synagogue unencumbered and open to the experience as soon as I had acknowledged my own shortcomings. I thought that ignorance was my *only* Jewish baggage. I did not understand how burdened I still was by ambivalence, ambiguity and rejection. Instead of coming to *shul* alone each Shabbat morning, I was bringing generations of Diaspora experience along with me, the distillation of centuries of learning from hardship and triumph, the lessons of growing up successful and Jewish in non-Jewish America—a distinctive and confusing legacy circumscribed by pride and prejudice.

Together, these forces contributed to my discomfort in synagogue and acute self-consciousness. Suddenly I was a gawky teenager all over again, wondering what tiny misstep would reveal to everyone that I didn't belong in this place which I wasn't really sure I wanted to belong to in the first place. The real challenge was to be treated as an adult learner, not as a kid learner. I knew about as much as an average ten-year-old, but I had the intellectual acuity and psychological complexity of an adult. I was one prickly, tender piece of ripe fruit—full of defenses, ready for harvesting but easy to bruise.

A Service Filled with Stumbling Blocks

Within months after I started regularly attending Shabbat services, I felt like I was making genuine headway addressing what I needed to resolve. I had come clean with myself and begun to understand the prejudices I had against worship—the ones I had been taught, the ones I had acquired all by myself, and the ones I needed to get rid of. I was beginning to feel at home in the sanctuary, but my progress seemed to occur *despite* the way services were conducted. I learned something each week when I read the English translations of the Torah and Haftarah portions and the commentaries, but that could just have easily taken place at home. I learned something when I heard a well-conceived sermon. I *felt* something simply being in community as I had these experiences. And yet it was not good enough. I stood in synagogue week after week wanting to experience the wondrous embrace of Judaism, and the service didn't even meet me halfway.

If the rabbis were so worried about the future of the synagogue and of Judaism, I wondered, why they weren't paying more attention to people like me? We *are* the future. There had to be hundreds, if not thousands, of Jews like me sitting in sanctuaries (either voluntarily or involuntarily) all over the country every Shabbat morning. Every time we're neglected, I thought, the collective future of our people is neglected. We needed to be taught to understand what everyone else was doing so that eventually we could do it too. Time should be spent explaining the rhythm and rituals of the service—such as dressing and undressing the Torah scrolls or the meaning and history of various songs and prayers. There should be discussions about what kind of space the sanctuary is supposed to be or the significance of its many decorative elements, an analysis of key Hebrew words in the liturgy or a dynamic interactive lesson about a Torah portion instead of a sermon about it. There should be regular discussions about current events and what Judaism has to say about them. *Something*—I didn't know what—should be changing in all of us during the communal worship experience. Being there *should* make a difference.

This wasn't a fugue on the tedious boomer complaint "But I came to synagogue *once* and nothing *happened* to me." I was putting in the time, and not expecting any form of instant spiritual gratification. I knew enough about the seriousness and complexity of what I was seeking to know that it *couldn't* be supplied on demand. I didn't come looking for something to be *done* to me. But I *was* looking for more than what I was getting. All of worship, I reasoned, should be an opportunity to learn and grow. It should be inviting, vital, enlivening, challenging. If we were *there,* the very audience the rabbis were always claiming to want, why were they neglecting us, the native strangers who were in their midst?

The prevailing assumption seemed to be that if you *were* there you should know what you were doing. I never knew what was coming next or why we were doing the things we were doing. It would have been so helpful to have a roadmap in the seat pocket, a basic guide to the structure and sequence of the service. Better yet, worship mentors should be available to sit with newcomers and gently guide them through the services. Without either one, the message was "Take it or leave it. If you were here regularly, like you're *supposed to be,* you'd understand and you'd feel like you were part of it." There was a subtle but unmistakable rebuke in the whole setup, maddening and humiliating at once.

Yet, I continued to attend out of a dogged conviction that the substance I sought *had* to be there or the institution wouldn't have lasted for thousands of years. Synagogues had certainly been around longer than Federations and UJA caucuses. I was sure there must be legitimate reasons for their longevity. All those Jews had to know *something!* Plus there was the fact that I am conservative by temperament—naturally attracted to reform, not revolution. By marrying a Conservative Jew, I had landed, entirely by luck, in the environment best suited to my sensibilities. The Orthodox approach, I thought, tended to require unquestioning acceptance of their version of tradition which violated my concept of emotional and intellectual autonomy. Inexplicably, to my way of thinking, they seemed to ignore modernity by refusing to acknowledge and incorporate the remarkable contributions of science, psychology, archaeology, feminism and technology into their system of belief. Reform Judaism, on the other hand, went too far in the other direction. It seemed to reject almost everything linked with tradition because it was either inconvenient, dogmatic, or undermined the sanctity of individual choice. This perspective seemed to sanction the dangerous excesses and indulgences of contemporary America: "If it feels good, do it." In search of community, I believed that the elevation of personal autonomy to a sacred entitlement seriously compromised the *possibility* of community. The Conservative movement, on the other hand, occupied the messy middle ground. It had the hardest time explaining itself because it was taking on the toughest job: trying to reconcile contemporary life with ancient precepts, balancing tradition and practice with modernity and necessity. I especially appreciated that the Conservative approach acknowledged the imperative of evolution. The rule of survival applies to every aspect of life: adapt or die. Of all the places where one might find God, I believe divinity is most likely to be discovered on the continuum of change. Four years later,

I am increasingly impatient with doctrine and all kinds of rigid denominational distinctions which are more often used to divide and
separate than to illuminate and unite. But as I began to seriously explore Judaism, I clung to the distinctions I understood to help guide
my choices and decisions.

All these inclinations and assumptions contributed to my persistent attendance in synagogue. I remained convinced that much of
what I sought from Judaism could be found there. And I had a growing sense that faith and intellectual rigor *could* coexist—that the latter did not necessarily preclude the former. But another factor was
at work as well. My resolve became a less significant factor as the act
of attending began to affect me. I found that I now woke to the alarm
clock on Saturday mornings with the desire to go to synagogue. I
didn't *have* to go anymore; I *wanted* to go. It was where I *belonged*.
It had become part of the rhythm of my week, and I was incomplete
without it.

I continued to work through some of my uneasiness with the
tension between the individual and community by laying claim to
this quiet time in the midst of community as something that was exclusively mine. I found sitting with friends distracting and moved to
the front of the sanctuary because I knew they would be less likely
to join me there. Increasingly, members introduced themselves to
me, particularly the older members of the congregation. I now knew
some of them by name and they made a point of greeting me each
Shabbat. "Darling," they would say, "it does my heart good to see
someone as pretty and young as you coming to *shul* each week."
(Never mind the pretty, it was thrilling to be told that forty-one is
young!) A few older men took shameless advantage of Shabbat,
greeting me by tapping their cheeks for a kiss or holding their arms
wide open for a hug. I willingly dispensed kisses and hugs. I was
gradually becoming an adopted member of the senior congregation,
and being made to feel important to them, as if their own children
were standing beside them.

Even though I felt a growing connection to the community, it
took me much longer to feel comfortable with the service. Now,
nearly four years later, I'm still working on it, occasionally getting

lost, and still ponderously wading my way through the Shabbat *Amidah*. (The *Amidah*, recited while standing, is comprised of nineteen blessings on weekdays, fewer on Shabbat, and is recited no fewer than four times on Shabbat.) I continue to stumble over the names of many of the prayers, struggle to remember what they're supposed to accomplish, and often mangle Hebrew pronunciations by accenting the wrong syllable. I do move now when I *daven* (pray), a comfortable rhythmic rocking reminiscent of the swaying motion I assume whenever I hold an infant. But I easily lose the rhythm because I haven't learned to attend to prayer the same way I do to babies. I don't always remember which way to turn if I'm handed a Torah from the ark. I have to stop and think whether I'm supposed to kiss the *siddur* (prayer book) first and then touch the Torah or the other way around. Sometimes I feel like the novice dancer in the veteran chorus line who's just one step out of sync with everyone else. Occasionally, it's funny; sometimes, it's mortifying. I never expected synagogue to be easy, but I did not expect it to take so long to acquire the confidence that comes with familiarity and growing mastery. Now I appreciate that there are no shortcuts to authentic worship. And there are moments when trust is the most significant asset you've got.

Trusting Tradition

Blindly at first, I trusted the tradition to explain itself to me. Much as I might resent it, I knew that sometimes I simply had to go through the motions. I would have to accept that not everything would "feel right" before I did it, and that if I withheld myself on the premise that I couldn't or wouldn't do something *until* it "felt right" I might never take any of the risks necessary to grow and learn.

Nowhere was this so evident as in my struggle with taking an *aliyah*, the honor of being called to the Torah to chant the blessings before and after a Torah reading. One Shabbat, only a month after I had started going to *shul*, the *gabbai*—the person who oversees the honors of reading from the Torah—offered me an *aliyah*. I turned him down immediately with a strained, polite smile and a reserved,

"Not today, thank you. But I appreciate your asking." Privately, I was fuming at my inability to get up and *do* it. When I shared the story with a wonderful Christian friend, he gently folded his hands in his lap, leaned forward and whispered sympathetically, "Lee, you *shouldn't* go up onto the *bimah* if it doesn't feel right for you."

I smiled, "Peter, that's Christian counsel and a Christian response." And we both laughed because it was true.

I was gleaning an entirely different message from my rabbi and my own experience. It was gradually registering through his sermons, his lessons, our conversations and my readings and time in *shul:* The point of going to synagogue was not *primarily* to get something out of it personally. Instead, it was to stand, to speak, to sit, to pray *in community.* If I didn't feel a communal spirit then I should go through the motions until I did. Even if I felt like a fraud ascending the steps to the *bimah,* I should climb them anyway. Sometimes doing—and doing again and again—preceded believing. This was the central lesson of the Sinaitic revelation: God expected us to do *before* we completely understood, to submit to divine will in faith even when reason or feelings would have us do otherwise. During High Holiday services in 1993, I was offered an *aliyah* again. This time I accepted the honor and when I stood before the ark, I felt overwhelming awe. I wanted to reach out and touch the breastplates, glittering against the scrolls. I wanted to smell the parchment, touch the wood finials, nuzzle the needlework. I wanted to experience Torah with my senses instead of my brain. Of course, I did none of these things. I behaved with absolute propriety. But I was gripping my *machzor* to keep my twitching fingers busy. Later that day, I asked a friend what the Hebrew letters mounted inside the ark meant. "Know before whom you stand," he said, "for you are standing in the presence of the Lord." Tears welled up involuntarily. I had actually *felt* the meaning—a gift I would never have received if I had continued claiming I had to wait to do it until I was "ready."

Three months later, I was delighted when I was offered another *aliyah.* I only bungled the next-to-last phrase because I refused to read the transliteration, wanting to chant the Hebrew using my newly acquired Hebrew reading skills. It was wonderful to be up there. I couldn't stop smiling. I belonged even though I didn't really know what I was doing. I was no longer an impostor who hadn't "earned the right" to be on the *bimah*. Instead, I felt as I ought to feel under the circumstances: joy at the honor of being called to the Torah, standing as someone who was entitled to be there because I understood the sanctity of the moment. I vowed as I came off the *bimah* that I would know what I was doing the next time I stood at the reading table, now that I felt I had the right to be there.

The final stage of my acclimation to the service was not just ascending the *bimah* but staying there for the duration. I became second vice president of the *shul* in June of 1994 and my new role as an officer called for regular "*bimah* duty." I was proud to be up there feeling so much a part of something I had recently felt so much outside of, knowing my comfort had been earned, not given to me. And it gave me a new role in the worship service: I wasn't being taken through it willy-nilly, but helping to take others through it. The order, the *seder*, began to reveal itself as I discovered that *I* was part of the order. I loved the moment when we turned back to the congregation after the Torah had first been taken out of the ark and sang the *Shema*, the central affirmation of Jewish faith. I looked over the sanctuary, smiled and thought, "This is *my* congregation, *my* community!"

Prayer was still a problem for me. I suspect it always will be. The truth is that I'm just not very good at it. After eighteen months of trying, I had made only minute progress, suspecting that true davening requires more than intent or *kavannah*, which is the correct spirit we should bring to the act. It also requires Hebrew literacy. I imagined that when the words left my mouth and I *knew* what I was saying, they would connect me with a place I could not yet name: A place that would make me whole with my past while grounding me firmly in the present. Until I made major inroads in my Hebrew comprehension, I knew that I would simply be going through the motions. Now, with the help of a teacher and hours of practice, I have acquired a modest fluency. With each passing week, davening comes more within my reach. Every once in a while, I discover to my amazement that I have actually davened a whole prayer. I am *in* the prayer, not outside of it. I am no longer performing the act; I *am the act.* Of course, consciousness immediately ruins the effect, but knowing that I *can* achieve it reassures me that at least I am headed in the right direction.

While all of us have the capacity to pray, the ability to pray takes regular practice to develop and retain. After four years of practice, I think of my religious spirit as a muscle that had atrophied with disuse. At the outset, it was flabby and poorly toned, so weak I could barely locate it. I realized that I prayed for the same reason I did sit-ups after the birth of each child. I could not feel my abdominal muscles even though I *knew* they were there; but I also knew that if I did the right exercises my body would eventually respond. Even though I had moments of despair, I stuck with it because the muscle tone I'd always enjoyed was not only a point of vanity, but necessary. As a sometime student of anatomy I knew that it was my abdomen, not my spine, that holds me erect as I walk through life. Likewise, I now understand that it is more my spirit than my intellect that enables me to stand up to life's challenges. I knew that cultivating my prayer skills would make me a better human being, a more complete Jew, and a person better equipped to make a difference in the world. Prayer is one of the best exercises I can use to locate and strengthen my spirit.

Leading an especially hectic life, I have come to appreciate that Jewish prayer is an act of quiet reflection and judgment. What happens if I truly turn inward and find nothing there? Kierkegaard defines despair as that state in which we are not even conscious there is a self because we have no sense of a connecting narrative in our lives. What narrative have I—the product of a conflicted Jewish legacy and a culture that celebrates autonomy yet trivializes privacy and personal dignity—been writing? The interplay between legacy and culture led me to construct a secularized ethnic shell around a spiritual vacuum. There wasn't room in me for God to enter—and prayer is one way we let God enter our lives. Would I dream of inviting a guest to visit if I wasn't home? Would I want a guest to visit if my house was a mess? I had to *be* home and I had to clean up for the visitor I most wanted to entertain. I'm still working hard on both.

Two years after I started attending synagogue, I was already beginning to forget who I had been when it seemed like such a brave and radical act to march myself into *shul.* I could barely recall how alien the service had felt to me. Unschooled and untrained, I had had to learn prayers I had never heard; learn about holidays whose names I could barely pronounce; figure out when to sit down and when to stand up by sneaking glances at my fellow congregants. I had to strain to recall when I did *not* know the melody to the opening of the *Amidah;* to remember how I had *pretended* to know the words and lip-synched or followed one word behind the congregation until the day I opened my mouth and all the words came out whole, on time and complete.

Now, I can barely remember how uncomfortable I had been at the spectacle of joy I witnessed during my first Simchat Torah service and how delighted I was to join in the dancing and celebration during my third; how I had reproached myself for despising the Purim service and its deliberate silliness, choosing instead to stand on the sidelines and judge my fellow congregants for their childish abandon while denying my own feelings of inadequacy; how foolish and self-conscious I had felt the first time I marched in the *lulav* (ceremonial "bouquet" made up of cuttings from willow, myrtle, and palm trees) procession, a grown adult carrying a bunch of branches around the *shul,* and how fulfilling and magical it seemed the fourth time around. My stomachaches were gone, artifacts of my inability to participate and understand. Now, I guard against the possibility of being co-opted by the familiarity and comfort I yearned for. I must not let my respect for tradition and convention, my desire to conform and belong, to conserve and preserve, overwhelm my inclination toward skepticism and constructive criticism.

I *have* discovered the community I sought. It resides at the absolute center of my congregation. It makes our sanctuary a holy place every time we gather to worship God and to affirm who we are as a people. Without it, our synagogue ceases to exist and becomes just another sprawling, well-maintained institution with admirable aspirations. My job as a member of the community is to remember clearly and honestly who I was so that I can help others begin to "get" the possibility that synagogue worship and celebration have the power to inform and transform their lives. My job is to find ways to help more people say they have found a home in synagogue. This profound *longing* for home grips so many of us, but, too often, we let ignorance, prejudice and pride prevent us from finding it. Instead, we scour the planet for other wisdom teachings, investigating and adopting eastern religions, or marginal or even fundamentalist versions of the western options, neither caring or daring to ask what teachings our own religious tradition might provide. As it turns out, all that we usually seek, we often possess from the start. We just need faith, courage, a heart and a brain to see it, admit it, hear it and begin to *do* it.

4

I Just Wanna Give My Kid a
Jewish Identity
(But You Gotta Get Your Own First)

*Get yourself a teacher, find someone to study with, and judge
everyone favorably.*

—Rabbi Joshua ben Perachya, *Pirke Avot* I:6

It was a relatively benign event: a birthday luncheon in honor of the
forty-fifth birthday of one of my friends. The only difficulty was the
time—Shabbat at 12:30. My growing sense of obligation to Saturday
as a day of worship and rest was making it increasingly problematic
for me to attend such events. Still, this was Vivian, the earthiest
woman I know, a woman at ease with her talents, her body, her life.
A convert to Judaism, she and her husband, Bob, had a remarkable
family of five talented, loving children. I admired her strength, her
convictions, and her friendship though our paths had crossed infre-
quently during the past few busy years of our lives. I was looking forward to a lunch that would be no more complicated than a happy
celebration.

There were seven of us at the restaurant table that late summer
day in 1993. I had arrived late, directly from synagogue. Slightly self-
conscious because of my tardiness, I moved quickly toward the space
saved for me at the table, and announced with a half-smile, "Been
praying," as I took my seat. We immediately launched into the free-
flowing conversation of women who have known each other for
years; women who have shared car pools, pregnancies, children's

clothes and secrets. Among us, we had twenty-one children. Most of them were around the same ages. Our talk buzzed around plans for the upcoming year; what child was going into what grade in which school; who was chairing what program in the community; who was looking forward to a new job or shift in work responsibilities. Suddenly, the conversation homed in on a topic that attracted all of us. One of the women, Karen, was recounting her ambivalence over forcing her daughter to go on with her religious education now that she was *bat mitzvah*. Carol conceded that she was having a similar problem with her son: "At fourteen, if he doesn't want to go I don't see how I can *make* him." Linda, whose children all attended day school through eighth grade and an enrichment program afterwards, stated that in her household her children's continuing Jewish education was a "given" and, therefore, "nonnegotiable."

"Fine for *you*," Carol replied, "but you don't have another whole schedule to deal with. What do you do when there's a football game that afternoon and an exam the next morning? Something has to give. And I know what will give in *my* house."

We all nodded sympathetically. This was a familiar dilemma. Karen, who well understood the vagaries of adolescent decision-making, proposed that the three mothers coerce their children into going by claiming that each of the *other* two children was going.

I was fascinated, but didn't participate in the discussion since I had previously eliminated the option for my two older sons and didn't feel entitled to put in my two cents' worth. I'd given the possibility scant consideration when, a couple of years before, Linda had raised with me the issue of Sam and Alex's continuing Jewish education. Now I felt remorseful because I had cut off that conversation so quickly, claiming that supplementary afternoon or evening programs made life too complicated for my kids and for me. It was a reflexive, almost thoughtless response on my part. I'd made the decision in a vacuum, void of any input but some thirdhand negative hearsay about the congregational high school program.

Now my views about everything Jewish were shifting and I was struggling to sort them out. I wondered out loud why this was so important to these women? Why were they spending even three minutes agonizing over it? What *difference* would it make in the long run? I posed the multiple challenge intentionally, placing the questions like a live grenade on the table. For a moment, no one spoke.

Then Carol replied, "How can you even *ask*, Lee? So that Jonathan won't be ignorant about his tradition. This is as important as learning biology. If only it weren't so damned inconvenient!"

"Well," said Karen, "because I want Kate to understand what I value about being Jewish, and why it matters to *me.*"

"And exactly *what* does everyone value?" I asked deliberately.

"Well, the values for one, and . . . and the holidays!"

"And what holidays *do* we all celebrate?" I queried a little more aggressively.

"Um . . . well, the High Holy Days and Passover."

"And that's it?" I snorted. "What's the message of value *there?*"

Someone else said that they demonstrated that they were Jewish to their children by the way they lived and the choices they made. I wanted to know how they chose which religious obligations to observe and which to overlook. I suggested that perhaps most of our Jewish choices had nothing to do with a sense of obligation. Maybe we were just looking for the least painless way to accomplish what was, for most of us, a burdensome task. I was itching for a direct confrontation. I wanted the whole Jewish mess out on the table along with our half-eaten meals.

Carol suddenly sighed in despair, "I just wanna give my kid a Jewish identity!"

"And how do you propose to do *that?*" I exploded. "You think you can just walk into a store and pick one out! Just take it off the rack? For God's sake, your kid doesn't get an identity in any other part of his life that way. What makes you think you can get away with it here? An identity isn't something you *give* to another human being. It's something you help them develop!"

My friends were stunned by my outburst and so was I. What happened to our pleasant little birthday party? Ambushed by my own passion, embarrassed by my anger, I avoided eye contact with my friends and looked down at the tablecloth. No one knew quite what to say. They were used to strong opinions from me, but I was not fond of making scenes. I was usually more reliable and level-headed than that.

Carol, stung by my angry words and direct assault, found a generosity in herself that I didn't deserve. She spoke up softly, "But how do I do that if I don't know enough myself?"

I answered irritably, "Damned if I know, but I have to do something. I can't just sit around talking about it or complaining about it any more. Life's too short and this is too important."

I took a breath and looked back up at my friends. "I'm sorry. I'm really sorry. I didn't mean to lose it that way. It's just that I'm so tired of all the posturing we do in the Jewish community! We claim to care about this stuff. And I think we actually do. But we're not willing to *do* anything about it. We want things done *to* or *for* our kids. We want to *purchase* their educations, *give* them identities just as long as it doesn't inconvenience us too much. We want everything for our *kids,* but nothing for *ourselves.* I don't think it will work that way any longer. We can't give our kids something *we* don't already have."

"Well," Linda opened in her familiar, comforting statesmanlike manner, "what do you suggest?"

The idea I had been toying with for five months since I had regularly started attending Shabbat services fully materialized in that instant and I spoke with a certainty that surprised me. "I want to study Torah. *Really* study Torah. I want to do it with a group of women. And I want to do it every week with a great teacher. The one thing I'm sure of from going to synagogue is that Torah is the heart of Judaism. If you don't know Torah, you don't know squat about Judaism and I . . . I don't know Torah. Is anyone interested?"

A moment of silence and then the stunning response: "I would do it." "I'd love it!" "I'd be interested." "Count me in!" We talked excitedly about days, times, places we might meet. All but one of us belonged to the same synagogue, and it seemed we might get permission to meet there. All that remained was to find ourselves a teacher. I volunteered to do the research and get back to them. Lunch ended on a celebratory note. My friends generously forgave my outburst, we sang "Happy Birthday" and parted with the promise that I would be in touch with them soon.

Getting the Right Teacher

I left the restaurant elated, feeling as if I'd accidentally stumbled upon a group of kindred spirits. This was odd considering the fact that all of us had belonged to a Jewish study group Linda and I had organized years before when our children were young. In fact, we were all together that day because of the relationships that group had engendered. I originally broached the possibility with Linda sixteen years before after hosting a Federation meeting in my home. As the speaker droned on, I wondered what would happen if some of the couples there came together to explore Judaism? This wouldn't be one of those *chavurah* groups I'd heard about where people conducted ersatz religious ceremonies, a bunch of amateurs masquerading as pseudo-rabbis, tossing flower petals into the air to symbolize manna as they worked themselves into a self-induced religious frenzy. I hadn't actually *witnessed* anything like that, but simply contemplating it gave me the creeps. It would be more like the study group my parents had participated in when I was a youngster. I had vivid memories of heated but amiable arguments in our living room over the Bible and other Jewish subjects. I would sit on the steps and eavesdrop on this contentious, opinionated, rollicking intellectual free-for-all that was punctuated with shouts and laughter. I savored the energy I detected on those evenings and the message that Judaism could so excite and engage adults.

Together, Linda and I had recruited seven couples who began meeting in 1979. Every six or eight weeks for the next seven years we met in one another's homes. We called ourselves *Kesherim,* Hebrew for "chain" or "link." Each meeting featured either a guest speaker, a guest topic taught by one of us, or a family-oriented celebration of a minor Jewish holiday. In our own way, we explored Judaism. One of the great sessions was taught by a local rabbi on death and grieving. The absolute nadir was a session I taught on the Holocaust. We made the fatal mistake of serving strawberry daiquiris at the start of the evening. By the time I'd reached the Nuremberg laws, people were sprawled on the floor, joking and giggling inappropriately. Disgusted, exasperated and slightly smashed myself, I asked for a resolution to make it a social evening and drop all pretense of learning. Everyone agreed and we had a party instead. Other efforts at teaching one another were usually disappointing. We simply lacked the requisite respect and authority to make it happen.

But we did have fun. We made a riotous movie to show to our children at our annual Purim party. One magical Sukkot at our home, we carved pumpkins, decorated gourds and made cranberry and popcorn strands to hang on the wooden frame that supported the canopy over our deck. We conducted religious ceremonies with prayers and rituals invented on the spot—almost as an apologetic afterthought: "We need a prayer. Does anyone have a prayer?" The most rigorous text we consulted was *The Jewish Catalogue*. It didn't *substitute* for the Bible; it *was* our Bible. Still we knew that, no matter how perfunctory or imperfect these celebrations were, our children were receiving the positive message that Jewish families come together to celebrate Jewish events and that they can have fun doing it.

The momentum for these gatherings eventually dissipated when we no longer had the needs of young families to satisfy. It seemed that, after all, we didn't have the energy or commitment for serious sustained study. So I never guessed that while a thirst for real learning was growing in me, so many of my friends were harboring a similar appetite. I had assumed I'd be doing this by myself for the rest of my life. In fact, I was beginning to reconcile myself to this possibility, using it to self-righteously set myself apart from people I knew "before" I started to take Judaism seriously and to align myself with those I knew "after." But even as I was nursing the distinction, I was not happy with it. It was a mini-melodrama I'd contrived to add a bit more virtue to my decision to seriously study Judaism. To discover that others whose friendship I already enjoyed, whose intellects I already respected wanted to join me was a gift . . . a true gift.

I called my rabbi, Joel Zaiman, to ask if he had any suggestions about who we might approach to teach us. He fired off a series of questions about the women involved and how serious I thought they might be: Who else might be interested? What did we want to study? What did I think we would accomplish? I was a little taken aback by the velocity and intensity of his questions. My request seemed simple enough: a group of women wanted to get together and study Torah. Why the interrogation? I regrouped and began again. I told him we wanted to study Torah, but we had no idea where to start. I claimed the group included both community and family leaders. I adamantly asserted it was *just* the kind of learning the mainstream Jewish community had to start engaging in if we were ever going to start *doing* something about Jewish continuity rather than simply talk about it. I could see a circle of influence beginning with this group and reaching out to touch our families, friends and assorted communal activities. I thought that ten to twelve members was just the right number and that they should all be women. I believed there was great value in a group of women studying Torah together since many women felt freer to take risks and to participate without men around.

When the rabbi called a week later, he got to the point immediately: "*I'd* like to do it."

"*You'll* teach us?" We had all heard his sermons and knew him to be a master teacher of unusual skill and talent. I hadn't even dared broach the possibility with him during my initial call because I knew how busy he was and didn't imagine he could take on yet another teaching obligation. "You're serious! You'll be our teacher?"

"Yes. I want to do it and we'll start with *Shemot* [the book of Exodus]. It's the beginning of our story as a people. *Bereshit* [Genesis] will come later." We agreed that the class would meet once a week for an hour between Sukkot and Pesach. I would recruit four other students to bring the group up to twelve.

A month later, we met for our first class. Twelve women walked in with new copies of the Jewish Publication Society's English translation of the *Tanakh,* the collection of Jewish sacred texts that includes the Five Books of Moses, the Prophets and the books known as Writings, and we started to learn together. Had each of us been asked what we expected from the year ahead, I imagine the response would have been reasonably consistent: to learn something about studying Torah, to grow from learning with each other and the rabbi, and to study whatever he wanted to teach us.

We weren't malleable or impressionable in the same way as younger students; each of us brought to the class a lifetime of knowledge and experience, and our eagerness to learn had the intensity and seasoned determination peculiar to adult learners. Almost from the start, we realized that the knowledge and exposure we brought was valuable in terms of who we were, but irrelevant in terms of what we were doing. It turned out none of us knew how to study Torah the way Rabbi Zaiman was going to teach us: Word by word and verse by verse. We all showed up at our first class in October with the kosher lunches we had agreed to bring. This was to follow the classic "lunch and learn" model. What we hadn't anticipated was the virtual torrent of words and ideas Rabbi Zaiman would unleash on us. His command of text and context, his easy authority with his knowledge, his electric energy as a teacher were so overwhelming that our fingers ached from note-taking. No one ate real food that day. We never brought lunches again. Within a month, the text was becoming meaningful for each of us in a different way.

For me, the story of the Exodus was coming alive. Not as a Cecil B. De Mille extravaganza with Charlton Heston striding around in a brown toga behaving as if God had actually approved the casting choice, but as a story of progressive development for Moses, the individual, and Israel, the people. The confrontation between Moses and Pharaoh became a theological struggle instead of a political powerplay, and the stakes were life itself. Because I was learning to read the text in a new way, I occasionally got lost that year while reading the Shabbat morning Torah portion. Simply forgetting where I was, I became immersed in the story itself, blazing with new ideas about leadership, peoplehood and God.

Reading Ourselves into Torah

One Shabbat, I didn't pray at all. I couldn't. The sanctuary, the congregation, the service all disappeared as I entered into Exodus and watched Moses return to Pharaoh, demonstrating again and again the increasingly devastating reach of God's power, until even Pharaoh's ministers counseled capitulation. I suddenly saw the last plague—the slaying of the first-born—as the moment of choice for the Chosen People. God couldn't pull this off without their active cooperation. The People couldn't be redeemed unless they were willing to mark their doorposts and slaughter lambs (a huge risk in a host culture that considered sheep sacred). In Judaism, redemption was *not* a passive activity. I saw how the story perched us on the threshold of the spectacular move from an oral to a written tradition and the transformative effect that transition would have on the people of Israel. I saw how Moses' isolation from his people prepared him for leadership and sympathized with the self-doubt that plagued him. His questions seemed appropriately fearful. How can I take this upon myself? What will sustain *me?* How will I know that what I am doing is right? I noted God's impatience with self doubt in the presence of revelation and divine selection and realized that, in Judaism, faith and leadership go hand in hand. My mind was teeming with questions and insights, and the knitting together of theology with story.   8/31/18

By the time we gathered for our last class in April, we had covered the first ten chapters of Exodus and understood we had merely scratched their surface. What we studied that first year is not as important as how we studied and its effect on us. We had been introduced, virtual novices all, to the world of Torah. In what was by no means intended to be an exhaustive survey of biblical scholarship techniques or an in-depth exploration of Exodus, Rabbi Zaiman had exposed us to various methodologies that gave us a sounder, more complex understanding of Torah, not only to read meaning *out* of it, exegesis, but to begin to find legitimate ways to read ourselves *in* to it, isogesis.

The experience influenced each of us differently. I knew when I listened to Rabbi Zaiman and a woman fluent in Hebrew argue over the nuances of certain translations, that, if I ever really wanted to study Torah, I would have to know biblical Hebrew. So I began to study Hebrew. For many of us, the study group triggered the first spontaneous family conversations we ever had about the Bible. Most of us had sophisticated literary tastes and knowledge so we responded enthusiastically to scholarly articles which profiled alternative ways to approach the Bible as canonized literature. We had serious theological discussions about the drama and evolving relationship between God and the people Israel. We had provocative discussions about the purpose and nature of religion that produced an assignment to invent a new religion. I chose television as the "temple," talk show hosts as the "priests" and their guests as the "sacrificial offerings," but soon realized that my understanding of the purpose of religion was insufficient to complete the analogue. The exercise made me appreciate that the development of an authentic religious system is an organic communal process. Religions are worked out in the context of community; cults are invented by individuals most often operating outside of community. I could mimic the trappings of religion, but couldn't manufacture the essence by myself, which was probably the point Rabbi Zaiman was trying to make.

We discussed geography, biology, psychology, dietary laws, contemporary Jewish identity, and Christianity. Gradually, each of us emerged with a new reverence for the profundity of this sacred text. We began to believe it might one day be *our* sacred text in a way we had not previously thought possible. Now it was not only possible, but desirable. Torah was no longer irrelevant or inaccessible to us. It was too important to us to entrust to the rabbis alone for safe-keeping. We felt a new and urgent responsibility to learn how to guard it and transmit it ourselves.

We were making time for this in the midst of our very busy lives and gradually those who stayed came to see it as a highlight of their week. The readings were sometimes onerous, often dense. Most maddening of all, we would receive a handout—an article or a take-home test—labor over it at home, and never even refer to it during class. This was a model of study in which the student didn't work to satisfy the teacher or be the star student or impress her fellow students—but to satisfy herself. The result of our home-based work was private knowledge intended to augment our personal growth. We were gradually cultivating a personal appetite for sacred inquiry, a learning redefinition that charged us, challenged us, changed us.

At the conclusion of the first year, which coincided with the end of Pesach, we dispensed with study for our final class and shared stories about our *sedarim*. Each woman spoke of a new confidence, a new sense of purpose, a new level of commitment to the rituals of Pesach. We felt responsible for our *sedarim* in a way most of us had never experienced before. With humor and honesty, we shared our accomplishments and disappointments. The pro forma recitation of the same old boring *Haggadah* was enlivened when one woman broke from the text and helped her family look at the plagues as a progressive revelation of God's power and separation of the people Israel from all others. Others told of a distinctly feminist spin as they shared *midrashim* (the stories and interpretations that try to answer questions the terse biblical text raises) on the crucial roles of women in the story. Some even wanted to write their own *Haggadot* because the ones available were so disappointing. The universal criticism was that most *Haggadot* neglected to tell the full story of the Exodus—a particularly puzzling oversight since the telling of the story was a fundamental requirement of the *seder*. The assumption of the various authors and editors appeared to be that everyone already knew the story so it didn't need to be included in the fixed text. Our experience around our *seder* tables told us how grossly unwarranted that assumption was in late-twentieth-century America.

As we went around the room, the realization slowly dawned that what we had discovered was not only our entitlement but our *obligation* to teach our children, our spouses, our guests, our relatives. One year of study with a master teacher had spawned a dozen fledgling teachers and influenced at least a dozen families.

The second year, in response to our request to make the class more participatory, Rabbi Zaiman proposed studying the Joseph stories. He understood that the human element of the story would appeal to us and provide greater opportunities for full engagement with the text. We switched to a more demanding translation of Genesis which contained the Hebrew, a more traditional English translation, numerous commentaries and excurses. The level of discourse rose as our increasing confidence and skills enabled us to better challenge the rabbi and each another. We were learning to read between the lines, to truly understand *midrash*: not only to read and discuss traditional and contemporary *midrashim* but to contribute our own.

Rabbi Zaiman readily admitted when we stumped him, but chastised us when we were stepping too far outside the tradition to honor authenticity. Slowly, he enabled each of us to appreciate the system of commentary that supported the ongoing living encounter with Torah so essential to the continuing vitality of Judaism. Occasionally, he distributed articles to a student and asked her to teach it the following week.

We approached the Joseph stories as mothers, talking about parental favoritism and sibling jealousies. We wrestled with the traditional view of Joseph as a gifted dreamer who got a raw deal and the less flattering view of Joseph as an extraordinarily ambitious manipulator who turned every adversity into personal gain. We played the roles of Joseph's brothers as they argued over leaving him in the pit or killing him, and speculated about the origin of their hatred. We tried to see through Leah's weak eyes and to experience Rachel's embittered, barren beauty—to understand how their competing love for one man had undermined their sisterhood.

Our explorations raised new questions. Did Jacob secretly hate Joseph for reminding him so much of his beloved Rachel? What was Torah telling us about parental favoritism, sibling animosities and society's assumptions about the privileges of birth order? What later historical developments propelled Judah to the forefront of the story? If we were in Joseph's position, would we have introduced our own father to Pharaoh with deference or embarrassment? What was Torah telling us about the respect due our elders? Most significantly, was there a powerful lesson in the Joseph story about the temptations and dangers of assimilation that faced all diaspora Jews?

Seize the Day

We continued to grow both as students and as teachers. I began to incorporate biblical texts and themes when speaking to Jewish audiences on the issues of philanthropy and leadership. When I had the opportunity to teach several high school classes in two different institutions, I discovered a comfort with and delight in biblical text, feelings I hadn't had the year before. And we all reported regular and rewarding spillover of class discussions into family conversations.

By our third year, we had the tools to revisit the classic stories of our childhood and learn them all over again. We tackled Creation, Cain and Abel, the Tower of Babel and Noah. After studying them, I don't imagine that any of us views sexual intercourse, innocence, consciousness, ecological responsibility, Shabbat, sibling relationships or our own relationship with God as we once did. It is not possible to study the text as we did without having it affect the way you see yourself in the world. It is not possible to be the same Jew at the end of it as you were at the beginning.

I remember one moment in particular. It came late at night as I was reading the essays Rabbi Zaiman had assigned for class the next day. I had struggled through the first two and was ready to call it a night when I decided to give the last essay, a short piece by Phyllis Trible, a professor of sacred literature at Union Theological Seminary, a quick read. The ideas were so crisp, so clear, so obvious that I thought on one breath, "Now why didn't *I* think of that?!!" and on the second breath I realized I had encountered a specific form of genius. She had reworked the Creation myth in such a provocative way that it summoned forth a completely new reading for me.

I suddenly recalled Rabbi Zaiman's question from the previous week: "If the original *adham* ["human"—not "man"] is androgynous, what does it do to your notion of sexuality?" I didn't get it then. I leapt to the easy conclusion that each gender possesses a quality of the other's sexuality. Nothing revolutionary there. I used my knowledge of my masculine and feminine traits all the time. But Trible's provocative statement "Meanwhile, the words of the ancient poem as well as their context *proclaim sexuality originating in the unity of 'adham,'*" made me return to the rabbi's challenge anew. Connecting Trible's statement to the Jewish principle of marital intercourse as an ultimate expression of holiness raised a whole other question. What if the root of that Jewish principle was embedded in this notion of initial androgyny? Then it is only through intercourse that we might discover, however fleetingly, the absolute unity God intended when humanity was first created! Seated in marriage, intercourse might be the highest form of partnership in which the union of the two partners becomes a momentary sacred whole greater than the sum of the parts! If we were originally one creature, then this is the only way we could ever recover the essence of that experience and return to the bliss that existed before human disobedience introduced disharmony and strife into the world. It is a way in which we could be reunited with God's original intention, experience God's holy purpose. It could be viewed as God's gift to us, a miraculous artifact of that ancient moment. As these understandings wove together, my heart broke loose inside of me and my eyes brimmed with tears. What joy and miraculous insights studying Torah could bring!

In our fourth year, we continued with the Genesis stories but added a new twist. Rabbi Zaiman broke us into smaller study groups and we agreed to teach each other the stories of the *Akedah* (the binding of Isaac), Lot's daughters and Hagar. We discovered the great secret of the Rabbis: The greater joy was in the study, *not* in the teaching. We found we had developed authentic text-based skills and the ability to manipulate a growing number of sources. Buoyed by a new confidence, we experimented with our lessons. One group interviewed, Ted Koppel-style, Hagar, Sarah, Ishmael and an imaginary friend of Hagar's. Another did a survey contrasting traditional with contemporary views of the *Akedah*, and included a song exploring Sarah's faith and her relationship to God. The Lot group brought contemporary questions to the text and used multiple sources to suggest possible answers. I wrote an original *midrash* on Sarah's response to the *Akedah*. I imagined what she was thinking for the three days that Abraham and Isaac were gone and what role she might have played in the story. Using historical data unavailable to the Rabbis and *midrashim* from a range of sources, I wrote it out in the form of a memoir and ethical will she asked Eliezer to give to Isaac after her death. I never imagined at that birthday lunch four years earlier that Torah study would lead me or my friends to a place of such rewarding creativity.

Studying with my friends returned me to the excitement of serious study. It was like being reintroduced to a once-cherished activity

I had nearly forgotten and mistakenly believed I had outgrown. As soon as my appetite was reignited, I couldn't ignore it. The more I studied, the more I needed to study. So I studied whenever I could: late at night; while waiting in doctors' offices; sitting in car pool lines; walking on the treadmill; and sitting in synagogue on Shabbat when I probably should have been davening. At one point, my daughter, Josepha, dubbed me "Mrs. Akiva." We both laughed—she because she was delighted with her cleverness, me because I took special solace in the fact that Rabbi Akiva was also forty when he first began to study. I learned that I cannot be the kind of Jew I want to be without studying. I cannot know what God or Judaism expects of me unless I know our texts and our tradition.

More than anything else, this study experience has forever colored my expectations of Jewish learning. Every time I study with others now, I expect that I will learn something of value as long as I am able to listen. Every time, I hope that my expectations of excellence, rigor and authenticity will be met. I was blessed to "get" such a remarkable first teacher and to "find" such generous partners to study with. And I am acutely aware that I have provided a different kind of Jewish model for my children—I am doing what I want them to be doing. I am acquiring the identity I hope they will forge for themselves. I can't give it to them but I can give them a model to use for themselves.

Perhaps the most significant lesson is that dedication and intention alone are not always sufficient to get us to our destinations. I had known for a while that I *needed* to study Torah and that I would prefer to do it in with other women. I'm not sure how much longer I would have whined, procrastinated and deliberated had it not been for that luncheon with my friends. I suspect I might have waited for something to drop in my lap. I would have sighed hopelessly and helplessly, "I *just* wanna study Torah with a group of women." We never know what event or moment will galvanize us, forcing or calling us to act, but we do have to be prepared to take advantage of it when it occurs. Luck meets carpe diem; *bashert* (the Hebrew word for the sense of destiny that results whenever luck and fate collide) meets Jewish activism. The moments are rare and valuable. We have

almost

9/01/18

to learn to recognize and seize them. As Rabbi Tarfon said in *Pirke Avot*, "*The day is short. The task is great. The workers are lazy. The stakes are high. The employer—impatient! Time is fleeting. Now is eternal. Discipline yourself to attention for the alternative is despair.*"

5

Just Because *Mom* Goes to Synagogue, *We* Have to Go to Sunday School?

Teach your child Torah, a trade and how to swim.
                                        —*Kiddushim* 29a & 30b

My husband and I did not know this famous teaching from Talmud or the fact that it uses swimming as a euphemism for physical and political survival in a hostile world. But we did know that sending our children out into the world without swimming proficiency was tantamount to sending them out with a death warrant tacked to their tiny chests. In the America they knew—a world of summer camps, boats and pools—swimming *was* a survival skill that might actually save their lives one day. So we made certain that they were all competent swimmers by age five or six.

As for "a trade"? We made a conscious effort to expose them to a wide range of career options. We talked about our work with them, encouraged them to ask other adults about theirs and often took them to visit factories and businesses during our vacations.

But Torah? We didn't see Torah knowledge as equally crucial to their survival because we didn't see it as crucial to ours.

The contrast between our diligence in attending to our children's physical and intellectual growth and our casual treatment of their religious training didn't bother us at all. We had very little trouble making a decision when we contemplated their religious school education. The choice almost made itself: Our primary concern was taking care of a large, young family. Their religious training was

71

nearly an afterthought—a minor, secondary consideration. We wanted Sunday mornings for family time. We wanted lazy mornings with the entire family lolling around in bed or playing outside with the dogs. We wanted impromptu trips to the hardware store, spontaneous visits to the zoo, and private time for each of the children with their father because they had plenty of time with me during the week. Religious school interfered with what we felt was a higher priority: Time together as a family. Besides, we told ourselves, religious school education had been a waste of time for both of us: an exercise in uninspired teaching, and nearly useless learning. The only vital childhood religious education experience I had had was my fifth grade afternoon Bible Study group.

Drawing upon that experience, I arranged for private tutors to come to the house for an hour and a half each week to teach each of our children once they turned six. I was positive we were doing the right thing. They were all introduced to the Jewish calendar and major holidays, and had a basic sense of Jewish history and a rudimentary grasp of Hebrew. The fact that there were hardly ever any groans on tutoring day was an unexpected bonus. I was pleased with the efficient way I had taken care of their Jewish education and I was confident that their Jewish identity was assured. I did not stop to wonder at their meager exposure to worship and observance. They attended synagogue only on the High Holy Days, their own *bar mitzvah* and the *b'nai mitzvah* of their friends and our friends' children. Their single consistent Jewish experience was Friday night dinner frequently enjoyed with our large extended family. We always lit Shabbat candles and my father said his special *kiddush:* "We praise God for this symbol of joy and thank Him for the blessings of the past week and the pleasure of being together again." We also shared family meals around the High Holy Days and the two Passover *sedarim*— the first night with my family and the second night with Nelson's family. And there were all those Sukkot, Chanukah and Purim parties with the other members of *Kesherim.*

I thought our children enjoyed reasonably rich Jewish lives until I began to examine the content of my own and found it wanting. I realized then what an enormous disservice I had done them in their religious upbringing. My parents had taught me to be proud of being a Jew and that Judaism and community service were synonymous. But they had also taught me that we could set ourselves apart from the Jewish community for religious observance—and still remain *in* community. I now understand that it is not possible to have it both ways. Neither community nor the individual can tolerate that separation and remain meaningfully connected. I taught my children each of the three lessons—pride, service and separation—I had so carefully and dutifully learned. The challenge now was to undo the damage of the third.

Why Be Jewish at All?

Before the March 1993 Shabbat morning when I voluntarily went to *shul*, I had expressed my adult Jewishness, like so many other well-intentioned American Jews, mostly by being active in Federation. Pleasant and usually undemanding, Federation involvement served my Jewish social and emotional needs. It provided an instant community that connected me with other relatively young Jews who shared similar values and enabled us to feel good about the work we were doing together. We raised money and helped decide how to spend it. We taught other Jews how to raise money. We participated in committees, young leadership programs, campaign divisions and task forces and all knew that this was decent, valuable work.

What I began to question was not the value of the work itself. There was no question in my mind that it was good: building humane facilities for our Jewish elderly; stabilizing aging neighborhoods so that Jews and blacks could live peacefully next to each other; addressing Jewish drug and alcohol abuse and domestic violence; investing in formal and informal Jewish education; and supporting Israel. If we had learned nothing else from studying the Holocaust, we had learned this: no one was going to take care of the Jews but the Jews. This was our guiding principle and we believed in it with all our hearts. But after eighteen years of service, I was beginning to question how we justified all this hard work. Wringing our hands, we would claim that we were worried about the dreadful statistics on Jewish continuity and that we did what we did in the name of Jewish survival. We commissioned studies, initiated Federation/synagogue partnerships to examine the problem of continuity and then wondered why we continually spun our wheels, getting nowhere slowly, over a long period of time.

The reason for the impasse became clear to me as I attended a plenary session on Jewish continuity during the 1991 Council of Jewish Federations General Assembly in Baltimore. In this particular session, Arnold Eisen, a professor of Jewish Studies at Stanford University, Barry Schrage, the executive director of the Boston Federation, and Joy Levitt, a Reconstructionist rabbi from Connecticut, eloquently laid out the continuity problem and proposed a range of solutions. I listened carefully, gradually realizing how empty my own life was in genuine Jewish content. I studied the avid expressions of everyone around me. They were eating this stuff up! And I waited and waited for someone to question the core assumptions that held our entire enterprise together: Why did it matter at all? Who *cared* if there were Jews around in 2010? Why *shouldn't* we go the way of other ancient cultures? Pack up our tents and disappear quietly into the sunset? That's what happened to the Greeks, the Romans, the Incas. What was all the kicking and fussing about? Why be Jewish *at all?* And why did everyone behave as though the answers to these questions were self-evident?

I scanned the rows of nodding heads and realized that few of the Jewish leaders assembled here *could* answer these questions, and that was why the professionals didn't pose them to begin with. I knew they couldn't answer them because *I* couldn't answer them— and *I* was a Jewish leader. I had bought the whole ideological package: salvation and survival lay in federation; it lay in civil Judaism, not in religious Judaism. Yet civil Judaism had not prepared me to answer the heretical questions that were suddenly making such a racket in my brain: *Why* did Jewish survival matter? And how could we possibly find the answer to that question among Jews who felt that the best—and, in many cases, the *only*—expression of who they were as Jews was through Federation activity? The activity itself *begged both questions* since we were all part of a closed system in which federation became the purpose of federation. We might invoke an almost sacred phrase—"We are one." Or we might borrow a particularly pithy quote from Talmud or Torah or *Pirke Avot*—"As our fathers sowed for us so shall we sow for our children," for campaign marketing purposes or to help us capitalize on the latest Jewish crisis.

But we couldn't *really* talk about Jewish survival because it was an insolvable problem for too many of us. Men and women who had passionately devoted their lives to this secular expression of Jewish identity had *not* planted in their children a commensurate passion sufficient to make them want to choose Jewish mates, set up Jewish homes and build deeply committed Jewish lives. Intermarriage had paid a call on all of our families. I no longer saw this as an intriguing sociological phenomenon or as a circumstantial byproduct of an enlightened modern commitment to diversity. It was irrefutable proof of one generation's inability to pass onto the next compelling reasons to *be* Jewish. We were the first generation of American Jews to be raised on a primarily secular diet. Like Chinese food, it was briefly satisfying, but as soon as we got up from the table we were hungry again.

Changing My Mind and Changing Our Plans

My parents' generation's formula of secular dedication was not powerful or persuasive enough for us, their children, to anchor a life around. Their conviction that Jews ought to survive was not related in any substantive way to specific Jewish concepts that merited our passion and attention. Although we had fulfilled our immigrant mission of achieving economic success and political freedom, our achievements had come at a cost. America had loved us to death and somewhere in the course of this love affair we had betrayed our forefathers. Underneath our frantic Jewish communal activities was a layer of residual guilt: we had abandoned almost everything our ancestors treasured in pursuit of not holiness—but the American dream. What amazed me was how many ways we tried to avoid confronting this terribly unpleasant truth. And suddenly I knew I was in line to create some new ways of my own unless I stopped deluding myself.

This wasn't an epiphany; I didn't leave that meeting with a fully conceived plan for discovering all that I needed to know to be a Jew who *could* answer these questions. But I did leave resolved to begin the process. I began by working with my siblings on the Jewish education project which, fourteen months later, led to my attending synagogue. Soon after that, I decided we needed to enroll our two younger children in Chizuk Amuno's three-day-a-week religious school. I brought up the subject of their Jewish education at dinner over several months. I tried to feign nonchalance, because it seemed like a good strategy, but I couldn't pull it off. I was about as subtle as a bull elephant on a rampage. The truth was I thought it was a matter of critical urgency, and I knew I was up against powerful conditioned behavior and family history. This was *not* the way we had always done it. I heard the annoyed whispers around the table: "Why do we have to change *our* life, just to satisfy Mom's latest and greatest passion? Maybe, if we're all *very* quiet or pretend to *humor* her, she'll get over it."

When a steady campaign of persuasion, lecturing and pleading didn't work, I simply *bullied* Nelson into agreeing that the girls should go to Hebrew school. It worked for the simple reason that he wasn't as opposed to it as I was in favor of it. So I won, but by default. Finally, I corralled our daughters and took them for an "interview" with Rabbi Stuart Seltzer, principal of the synagogue's religious school. Ostensibly, this was a preliminary conversation intended to help them learn about the school and for the principal to assess them. But the girls knew it was a set-up. They had a fine time with the rabbi who put them at their ease. When I returned to pick them up from his office, they were both smiling.

As we walked out of the building, Lindsay said, "Nice meeting, Mom. But do we really have a choice?"

Josie kicked a pebble, then a stone, then the curb (which I considered preferable to my shin) and groused as we got into the car, "Yeah, just because *Mom* goes to synagogue, *we* have to go to religious school!" I hauled out all my old dinner table arguments: I had deprived them of learning and worshiping in community, and they would never understand the most basic principles of Judaism without that kind of communal exposure. I'd neglected a crucial component of their education and would be abdicating my responsibility as a parent if I continued to neglect it.

"What about *Dad?*" Josie asked. "What does *he* think?"

"He doesn't think it's as important as I do, but he's willing to try this year as an experiment."

"And if we don't like it?" they asked in stereo, a little too hopefully.

"As far as Dad's concerned, you won't have to keep going. As far as I'm concerned, you will. We'll just try to deal with what you don't like."

It was the first time the kids saw us as a divided camp, and they played us off, one against the other, as skillfully as any kid intent on getting their way will do. The war was on. The girls were clever and persistent and quickly recruited a willing ally in Nelson. The conflict was especially unpleasant and difficult because this was the first time Nelson and I had ever disagreed over something important regarding our children. The kids were getting two different versions of reality from parents they loved and admired. No one doubted my resolve, but they never fathomed its depth. Nor did I anticipate the intensity of their resistance. The following journal entries illustrate our family's frustrations over three years.

10/17/93

Showdown. The worst kind: when parents are genuinely at odds over something important and the kids know it. Overwhelmed with work, Nelson is cranky, looking for something to lash out at. We all caught it this morning. He told the girls while driving them to religious school that he resented the time it took away from them and him. This was all Josie needed to tell him how much she hated it, how boring and repetitive it is. And this is after she's attended ten classes. He returned home, decreeing we would discuss "this whole Hebrew school thing" after the girls finished school that day. I figured he'd had his shot with the girls so I had mine when I picked them up and told them once again that we had made a terrible mistake by not sending the boys to religious school and I was determined not to repeat it with them. This was as important as their elementary school education. And it was equally nonnegotiable.

When I got home, I was firm with Nelson. I insisted that their education could not be achieved at his convenience. He still had trouble seeing it although he agreed that one month was not a fair test of anything. The real problem is that he cannot really say what Judaism means to him while I am learning to clearly articulate what it means to me. I told him I wanted them to learn what is beautiful, charming and imperative about Judaism. I want them to know the language, to respect Torah, to begin to understand how Judaism should guide their lives. He maintains it doesn't guide his life at all. A declaration which stunned me especially since I know it isn't true.

At bedtime, Josie hugged me and said, "Mommy, I'm sorry for being so difficult about all this."

"I appreciate your apology, Josie. Do you understand why I think this is so important?"

"Yes. So I will know what's important about being Jewish and understand what I have to sacrifice."

"Sacrifice?"

"Yeah, you know. My time. My valuable time. Special mornings with Dad."

"True, Josie. Everything we do has consequences. But there are also some wonderful things. Learning a new language. Understanding special holidays."

"Sitting in boring synagogue for three hours listening to those people sing and big old Rabbi Zaiman talk, talk, talk."

"Things are often boring when we don't understand them because we can't participate fully."

"I know. I know. And I'll learn how to participate by going to Sunday school."

"Well, partly. We haven't gotten to the next part yet."

"Oh, no! You mean next I have to go to services with you?"

"Yep. Not right away, but sometime this year."

A devilish grin: "I can wait!"

A year later, not much had been resolved:

9/11/94

Today was Josie's first Sunday school session for the year and the occasion for a major clash of will between me and her over how religious school has taken up "all" her free time. The issue, as she states it, is, "Who is in charge of my life?" She accuses me of not giving her enough credit for making sound judgments. She doesn't have enough control over her life. I have too much. There were tears and shouts of "I won't go and *you* can't make me. They don't teach us anything worth knowing and even when they do they treat us as if we're stupid babies!"

There is enough truth in this to make me uncomfortable. "I'm sure that part of what you say is true. I do have lots of control over your life. That's my job right now. I use my judgment about the things you ought to be exposed to. Even though some of them may make you unhappy, I'm still going to insist that you do them because I love you and I believe they're in your best interest. I know I can't control how you react to these things but I can be in charge of whether or not you are there. You *are* going to religious school this morning and you *do* have a choice. I can take you in your pajamas or in your school clothes. I can carry you to the car kicking and screaming or you can walk. You can go crying or smiling. You have a lot of choices to make in the next ten minutes. I'll wait for you in the front hall."

Josie came down in five minutes, sullen but dressed. I hate these scenes. I know all this would work so much more smoothly if I had Nelson's support rather than his grudging acquiescence. I am afraid of what my insistence will breed: unfair hostility toward me but also, much more worrisome, Judaism itself might become the whipping boy for everyone's accumulated resentments. I've tried all the arguments that make sense to me: "Sweetheart, if the kids told us they didn't want to learn how to read, would we say that's fine, it just gives you more time to spend with me?" Or "We don't neglect their bodies. We wouldn't dream of neglecting their intellects. Do their souls need any less attention?" Or "We send them to school to learn the history of their country. Why shouldn't we send them to school to learn the history of their people?" And finally, "We want them to be literate citizens. Don't we want them to be literate Jews as well?"

Just last night we talked about the difference between Jewish monotheism and other religious theologies. *Our* God expects something of us. Our God wants a certain kind of behavior from us—to attempt to *be* like God, to *become* holy. Other gods require adulation and obedience, not emulation. Nelson seemed so excited by these ideas! They made the concept of God useful instead of a delusional form of superstitious thinking. Something worthwhile to aim for. And now, ten hours later, our youngest daughter is staging a major hissy fit in the front hall while he sits within earshot, placidly reading the paper in the kitchen. She knows that's one of the reasons she can get away with it.

The wonderful irony is that Josie emerged from school smiling. "My teacher is weird. She speaks in Hebrew and then writes the words on the board and we're supposed to understand them. It's really weird." A little later came a sheepish confession: "I really like my teacher. She's spontaneous and funny. I had a good time today." Of course, she tells Nelson that it was just the same old boring stuff all over again.

Twenty months later there was another assault. This one was more subtle than Josie's since it came from her fourteen-year-old sister, Lindsay.

6/18/96
We went to the ball game tonight. It was fun—the first time the entire family had been together since Pesach. We left the stadium when it started to rain, all piling into Nelson's massive Chevy Suburban, enjoying the happy tumult of three different conversations going on at once when I heard a snippet of conversation from the back of the car.

"It's not fair. It really isn't. She didn't make *you* do it." This was Lindsay in the rear seat talking to the boys.

"Well, if *she* gets out of it, I'm not going to do it when it's my turn!" Josie announced from the middle of the car.

"What's not fair?" I asked without turning around.

"That I have to go to that stupid *Chavurah* program again where I don't learn anything except how to waste two hours. Alex didn't have to go at all and you let Sam quit." I thought Lindsay and I had settled this weeks ago when we agreed she would commit to another year of study one evening a week at the *shul*. I suspected that she was bringing this up now because she could count on reinforcements.

"It *was* pretty stupid, Mom," said Sam who had joined a *shul*-sponsored Jewish book club when he was a junior in high school and quit after a few months. "A bunch of kids sitting around talking about books they hadn't even read. It was nothing but a mid-week social hour."

I felt the beginning of a panicky despair. I was outnumbered and didn't know enough about Lindsay's program to properly defend it. Rabbi Camras had given me the syllabus and text for the course, but I'd only glanced at them.

"Really, Mom," stated Lindsay, "it *is* a ridiculous waste of my time. I'm going into high school next year. The work load is going to be heavier. I'm going to be playing three sports. We spent this whole year in *Chavurah* on a bunch of philosophers whose names I can't pronounce and I can't remember one class that was good. I haven't learned one thing!"

Then Nelson blurted out, "That's it. I've had it! I don't want my daughter away from me for dinner during the week. I hardly get to see her as it is. School is more important now. She's got to start preparing for college."

"And what's all the rest of her life been," I fumed silently, "a dress rehearsal?" I was suddenly grateful for the dark, the rain, the relative seclusion of the front passenger seat in this great barge of a car. Everyone was waiting for my response. I drew in a breath, pushed away all my frustration, hurt and anger and responded.

"I've already paid for the class and sent in the contract. And, Lindsay, you agreed because you were getting moved up another grade."

"Is that true, Lindsay?" Nelson asked.

"Yes but . . ."

"No 'yes buts.' It's settled. You made a commitment. You
have to keep it."

I swallowed my tears, noting the ache in my gut. Why had I
failed so miserably to convey the urgency of all this to my own
family? How could I travel around the country preaching about
these things to others, yet be so unsuccessful at bringing them
into my own home? It's so painful to acknowledge that there is
no easy solution to this problem. I simply have to stay the course
and insist on what I know is right. What I really want is not victory, but unanimous consensus that this is the right—and the
best—thing to do.

Sending the kids to religious school has had its moments of joy.
If Josie hadn't been in religious school, she would never have said,
as if stating the most self-evident truth in the world, "Exodus is *not*
a bedtime story, Mom!" when I tried one night to pass it off as one.
Lindsay would not have approached Nelson and me three months
before her *bat mitzvah* to ask us to learn to chant Torah because she
wanted us to take part in her service, and I might *still* be merely
thinking about learning to read trope (the notes for chanting Torah
and Haftarah). We would not have a *tzedakah* box in our dining
room now if it wasn't for the *mitzvah* program that required each
child and family to take on a new *mitzvah* during the *b'nai mitzvah*
year, part of Lindsay's seventh grade program. I would not have had
the chance to turn to my children for help as I labored over the Hebrew alphabet and struggled with new words.

Can Religious School Be "Cool"?

I do not dismiss my children's claims that they are bored or infantilized, even though they attend one of the more enlightened, progressive religious schools in the nation. There aren't enough
moments like the one when Josie dove into the car exclaiming,
"That was the *best* day! We had so much fun!" and described in
detail building a miniature *sukkah without* adult intervention. The

enthusiasm carried well into dinner where we decided that next year *we* would build a *sukkah.* The thrill of discovery was still there even as I put her to bed hours later. "Remember. Next year, Mom. Our own *sukkah.*" I smiled, kissed her on the forehead and remembered my own Sunday school bookends.

Rare moments like these make me wonder if we need to throw out the entire religious school curriculum and start from scratch based on what we know about cognitive development and effective pedagogy. It is even more imperative to do this when most Jewish kids can only dedicate time *outside* of their secular school schedules to their Jewish education. Maybe we need to question all our assumptions about basic Jewish literacy. If this formula didn't work so well with my generation, why are we essentially repeating it with minor modifications? We're tinkering, when we should be redesigning. Maybe if we truly believe in the Jewish principle of lifelong learning and promote *that* from each child's first educational encounter we could do things differently. We could eliminate the old challenge—trying to cram in as much information as possible before age thirteen—and undertake an entire new set of challenges. How do we want kids to think Jewishly? How do we want their learning to reflect their Jewishness? If we know what kinds of questions we want them to ask and what kinds of problems we want them to confidently confront, then we could restructure the whole experience so that they could graduate with their curiosity and enthusiasm intact.   9/02/18

Other wonderful things have emerged as well: We have all learned to compromise. The schedules we operate under as a family are grueling and sometimes truly antithetical to healthy relationships. Resistance to the lost time with Dad was not only the real lost time with Dad but simply the *possibility* of all that might be done with Dad if the time were *there.* In imposing an inviolate Sunday routine on our lives, I had taken away even the fantasy—a whole lazy day stretching before us with nothing to *do* except to enjoy the pleasure of one another's company. (Forget, for the moment, that if we backed up a day there probably isn't a better description of what Shabbat could mean to our family if we actually observed it). So we cut a deal. Josie and Nelson get to choose one Sunday a month for her to skip Sunday school so they can be together. The only requirement is that it has to be planned in advance. And Nelson thinks he has finally discovered why religious school was invented in the first place.

One Sunday, three winters ago, he offered to take the girls to school at 9:00 A.M. to let me sleep in. I dozed off only to be awakened as he slipped in beside me whispering, "Alex is still asleep, the girls are in school, the dogs are fed and I took the phone off the hook." I needed no further explanation. Afterwards, he sighed contentedly, *"Now* I know what Sunday school is for. The only problem is," he mused, looking up at the ceiling, "what to do next year when Lindsay's not in school anymore?"

"That, darling, is what *Chavurah* is for!"

We are all inching our way toward agreeing on the necessity of the children's religious education if not on the precise form it should take. The boys have a standing requirement (imposed by me) to take two Jewish Studies courses before graduating from college. Sam has become a little involved in the Center for Jewish Life at Princeton, has exceeded my minimum Jewish studies requirement and plans to write his senior thesis on the political behavior of American Jews. Alex agreed to go to a few Hillel activities during his first few months as a freshman at Duke University. "I'll give it a try, Mom" was the only promise he could make, but the promise itself was a small victory. As a junior, he voluntarily enrolled in an additional religion course beyond my requirement because he found the subject so engrossing, and he began to attend Hillel Friday night services on a routine basis. Lindsay did participate for one and a half years in the much-maligned *Chavurah* program that meets every Tuesday evening for two hours. Although she dropped out in the middle of the second year and refused to go back the third year, she is considering the possibility of a high school summer trip to Israel. And Josie, who begins sixth grade this year, will participate for the second year in a special program that teaches trope, the notes for chanting Torah and Haftarah, and requires attendance at Shabbat services twice a month. When she asked what I thought of the idea, I mused that it might make studying for her *bat mitzvah* much easier. Fortunately, she landed in a class with several friends who think religious school is "cool." Sometimes peer pressure is a good thing.

During a recent question-and-answer session following a speech I gave, I was asked, "What guarantee do you have that your children will all be practicing Jews fifteen years from now?"

It took a moment for me to understand that people might actually expect guarantees with their children. "There *are* no guarantees. I figure there's a fifty-fifty chance that they might—or they might not. But whatever it is, at least I won't be saying, 'I wish I had been clearer about what I was doing and why.' I won't be wondering if I could have set a better example, or chastising myself for teaching my kids to do as I say and not as I do. I'll know that I gave it my best effort and that's all any parent can ever hope to do with their kids."

Last year, I asked my friend, Linda, why she hadn't tried harder to convince me to pay attention to all of this. She looked at me with surprise, then said, "Lee, I *did!* You don't remember it, but I've been talking with you for years about this. You just weren't ready to *listen.*"

I asked Rabbi Zaiman the same question. He wasn't quite as gentle, but the question did amuse him. "Give me a break! Try to convince *you* of something you don't believe in? I spend my time working on things that have a possibility of happening, not hoping for miracles. I'm a rabbi, not a prophet." We both laughed.

My rabbi and friend were both speaking the truth. I *was* that unapproachable person who congratulated myself on solving the problem of my children's religious education with such painless efficiency. I *was* that misguided woman who rushed with confidence to do harm to my children. I *was* that young mother who drove past the congregation on Sunday mornings, my van filled with kids on the way to some other destination, thrilled that I didn't have to queue up for yet another carpool line.

I came late to the understanding that parents have the obligation to teach their children Torah, a trade and how to swim. It seems that our sages were wiser about survival skills than are many American

Jews. They knew *all* that a child required in order to "make it" in the world. Sadly, most of us only take care of providing the last two requirements for our children. But of one thing I am absolutely certain: our tradition teaches that it's never too late to go after the first . . . either as a child or as a parent.

9/03/18

6

What I Know Now I Could Put in a Thimble; What I Knew Then I Could Put on the Head of a Pin

She is a tree of life to all . . . who hold fast to her.

—Proverbs 3:18

As I started my journey into Judaism, I knew what I knew . . . which wasn't much. Learning more wasn't worth either my time or my energy. After all, wasn't Jewish education that spiritless and mechanistic experience I remembered from my Sunday school days? And didn't I know enough to get by in terms of the life I had chosen for myself? The fact that I didn't know the difference between Shavuot and Simchat Torah didn't bother me because, as far as I was concerned, neither holiday was important. The fact that I only attended synagogue under duress seemed a reasonable reaction to what was consistently, for me, a spectacularly boring experience. The fact that I couldn't read Hebrew didn't limit me in any way. Why did I need Hebrew if I didn't pray and had no plans to move to Israel? The fact that I didn't know there was a formula to the Torah readings or a rhythm to the Jewish year apart from the "major" holidays (Rosh Hashanah, Yom Kippur and Pesach) didn't matter because my life had its own formulas and rhythm that reflected my commitment to family and community. These rationalizations worked as long as my definition of what it meant to be Jewish remained essentially secular. When that definition shifted, everything else shifted as well, and my few little tidbits of knowledge tumbled off the head of the pin I had judged sufficient for holding all the Jewish knowledge I thought I ever needed to possess.

What I discovered is that, as far as Jewish knowledge goes, I had definitely *not* learned all I ever needed to know in kindergarten. To my dismay, even what I *thought* I had learned wasn't very useful, either. The hardest part was coming to acknowledge the enormity of my deficiency. Although I had passionately clung to the "Jewish" qualifier in my life—pick a role, any role, and put "Jewish" before it: funder, leader, mother, American—I finally had to admit that my use of the term was shallow and self-serving. It was a matter of convenience. My ignorance of all things Jewish was so vast that it was nearly stupefying, and my satisfaction with that ignorance was indefensible, especially if I wanted to continue to claim that *being* Jewish was at all unique, distinctive or essential—to myself, or to others.

Looking back, I don't know that I would do anything differently than I did. More importantly, I'm not sure that I *could* have. The path I chose reflects my personality, circumstances, opportunities and inclinations. I didn't have a methodical plan; back then, I certainly didn't have a metaphor for my predicament. I simply had an insatiable need that screamed for satisfaction. My "plan" was to feed the appetite and worry about metaphors later. Recalling the early stages of my journey, I am reminded of the plant in *Little Shop of Horrors* that grows and grows in the dark and demands to be fed in a louder, increasingly more imperative voice. Such a voice sometimes woke me in the middle of the night and sent me scurrying to my computer to record a new thought or question or to my growing library to lose myself in words and ideas. On some nights, the voice wouldn't let me go to sleep at all. For many months, I got by on three or four hours of sleep a night. Nelson often complained, and with good reason. So I climbed into bed with him, then "slipped out" after he fell asleep, feeling like an errant teenager sneaking off for an illicit rendezvous: Torah, my "lover," awaited me in the dark.

I spent many late night hours struggling with texts, commentaries, new ideas, new vocabulary. In the process, our Jewish library expanded from one tattered copy of James Michener's *The Source,* a King James edition of the Bible, the *Junior Jewish Encyclopedia* and the first and second editions of *The Jewish Catalogue* to more than three hundred Jewish books today. Many are gifts from friends and relatives; some came from my father-in-law's home after his death. Many I purchased myself. The most meaningful, however, came from teachers who influenced me at critical junctures with their choices. Each of their books came with the implicit message: "I have observed your journey and want to assist you. Here is a book you might find useful." One day, I will read all of these books. For a long time, however, I believed I had to read all of them in the same day and despaired that there would never be enough time to read and learn all I needed to know.

Torah as Fire

Occasionally, I wept with frustration at all the time I had dithered away while patting myself on the back for being such a "good" Jew. I grieved for all the lost time and lost opportunities, for all the important things I was sure I would have done differently if I had known *then* what I knew *now*. But while it was important to acknowledge my frustration and grief, I had to replace them with something more life-sustaining and purposeful. For me, study was the answer, although each person must choose his or her own way. I know now that it is possible to learn with a little more sanity and with much more balance. Gentler, steadier and slower would have been kinder to me and my family, but I almost totally lost touch with those qualities for a while. I wasn't the proverbial bull in the china shop since I always remembered that I was confronting *sacred* texts and *sacred* traditions and I treated those with the respect they deserved. I was more like a hound straining at the leash, howling to be let loose.

As I started to learn, a helpful metaphor for the experience emerged: We don't expect our baby blankets to grow with us. They're designed to cover our infant bodies and we leave them behind when we outgrow them. The pediatric version of Judaism I had was the educational equivalent of a baby blanket. I could continue to cling to it or I could drop it and go off in pursuit of something far more substantial and enduring to wrap around my adult body, mind and soul. Apart from love, it seems to me that only religion has this kind of power—the power to move and possess us so completely. It requires us to examine our practices, our beliefs, our hearts, our souls, our public self and our private self. When I speak with other adults who also chose to check their Jewish ignorance, I hear the same impassioned response. They describe an undeniably profound pull toward some thing they did not know existed—some primitive yet irresistible force. It is as if a slumbering giant awakened inside them and is now bellowing for his dinner.

Our Rabbis speak of Torah as life-giving—and they are correct. They never lose sight of the fact that Torah is God's gift to humanity, and to the Jewish people in particular. They explore its dangers, its wonders, its challenges. But they caution people *just like me*—the ones who have caught the passion, but have not yet mastered it—to exercise extreme care when approaching the hallowed arena of Torah study. "Fire: Close up to it, one is scorched; away from it one is chilled; near but not too near, one enjoys it. So are the words of Torah; as long as a man labors in them, they are life to him; but when he separates himself from them, they slay him" (Sifre Deuteronomy 343). They recognize Torah's seductive qualities and the intoxicating nature of its divine power. This recognition is only significant, of course, if you believe—if you *know,* as the Rabbis know—that God resides in Torah. After Sinai, Torah became the instrument of divine revelation. If you want to encounter God and know what God wants of you, then you must do what our sages suggest: go study Torah.

I did not understand this at first. I only began to feel Torah's gravitational pull as I sat through months of numbing Shabbat morning services. Only slowly did the centrality of Torah begin to register with me. The very thing I was looking for, the source of purpose and meaning, the anchor for my self-definition as a Jew, had been there all the time! Hardly anything in my background had prepared me to look *there* for answers to the questions I was asking: What does it mean to be a Jew? What must I *do* to be a Jew? How can I—and how must I—live as a Jew in America in the next century? Once I understood that Torah was *the* place to turn to, other things became clearer: I needed to study with a group. I needed to learn Hebrew. I needed to understand the Rabbinic tradition. I needed to understand *midrash* and commentary. So I approached a variety of teachers for guidance, and maddeningly the universal response was a Rabbinic one: They answered my question with a question.

"Where do *you* want to start? What do *you* want to learn?" Rabbi Zaiman said to me one afternoon, a few months after I'd started to attend services.

"Would you say that to a six-year-old who doesn't know how to read?" I shot back. "If I knew how to read, I wouldn't be asking for your advice! I'm so ignorant that *I don't know what I need to know.* I only know that I know almost nothing."

He smiled and leveled me with a dead-on stare. "*You* need to slow down. That's what you need to do."

"I can't. I just can't. I'm not in charge right now."

"Then proceed at your own risk and understand that it's risky business. Keep coming to services. Keep reading. The answers will become clear to you and then you'll know what you need to know."

"That's *not* the answer I was looking for."

"But it's the answer I'm prepared to give right now."

"And why should I trust it?"

"Because I've had *some* experience with these things. I've seen others as hungry as you. Slow down and trust more. It will all become clear."

I remained bewildered that all the people with authority kept dumping all the responsibility for my learning directly back into my lap. It seemed like a bureaucratic run-around. *Every* teacher I studied with or approached that first year was practicing the pedagogical principle to "meet the learner where she is." This principle acknowledges that when the learner's needs and situation are respectfully considered, powerful learning is more likely to occur because it takes place where the student "is," guaranteeing his or her investment and attention.

My teachers were acknowledging that I came to this new learning with a lifetime of experience, a set of skills, expertise in certain areas and a capacity to define what I wanted to achieve. All those assumptions were correct. What the principle did not take into account, however, was that I had virtually no experience with authentic Jewish learning and, therefore, no way to orient myself to its nearly overwhelming possibilities. Meeting me where I was *might* be desirable, but it ignored the fact that where I was was certainly not where I wanted to be—and that I had no way of knowing where I *should* be. I needed a frame of reference. Without that, the transformation would take place in a pedagogical void—a classroom of one which, of course, flies in the face of our tradition's many cautions against solitary study.

I learned that there are good reasons for those cautions. For a while, I was nearly consumed by the urgency of the yearning that drove me. I woke up aching for knowledge I didn't have. I went to sleep with my brain throbbing from all the effort to wrap myself around this vast, seemingly endless tradition that stretched back across the millennia. It beckoned me with an ineffable aroma that inflamed my senses and ignited my appetite. I smelled it at services; it spiraled up out of every Jewish book I opened: elusive, exotic, mouthwatering and full-bodied at once. I was embarrassed by the nakedness of my desire and I couldn't talk about it without getting a huge lump in my throat. I had no rational explanation for how or why this desire provoked such an intense emotional response. I finally realized that it was an involuntary response that I shouldn't apologize for and couldn't control. I needed Torah for the same reason that humankind needs fire: I couldn't live without it.

Milestones in Poetry

I surrendered my vanity, admitted I knew nothing and wanted to learn every Jewish thing anyone was willing to teach me. I began studying Hebrew with a tutor and studying Torah in groups and with individual teachers. I attended every course offered at my synagogue and many in the rest of the community. In the process, I discovered that my adult learning had milestones every bit as significant as the childhood learning milestones I had cherished or agonized over: the first book I ever read out loud, my first play, my first written story, my first research paper, the first teacher who helped shape my life. And I found an accompanying need to capture some of these milestones in poetry. Something about the intensity of these moments called for the precision and image-driven discipline of the poem. A friend laughed at my description of my first Hebrew lesson—how tough it was to learn a new language in middle age. After we finished chuckling, I realized that I had failed to convey the true wonder of what I was doing. There was nothing quite like it. I told her how it reminded me of the six-year-old I remembered being—the little girl who wriggled and squirmed at the unfamiliar, almost erotic sensation of intellectual stimulation and beginning mastery. I told her what a gift it was to find that kid again at age forty-one.

Learning Hebrew

Dumb and six at once
I am at forty-one.
Wrapping awkward tongue
around new sounds.
Setting strained eyes
on alien shapes.
Stolid, sturdy, stern on the page,
they silently reproach me for decades
of studied ignorance, proud denial.
I am humbled, intellect brought low
as I stoop to scurry under the words,
to know them without the painful
sounding out and putting together
of eye and voice.
I curse my stubborn brain—
too slow for
nimble desire.
Young work for an old learner.
Dumb and six at once.
I rail at my clumsiness,
delight in my ambition.
Knowing delight will prevail.

Mastery will come.
Meaning will follow.
I will begin to learn
how to be dumb and six at once . . .
and leave stiff frustration behind.

Months later, I wrote about a moment when I suddenly realized I was thinking in Hebrew. Due to time constraints and age, learning Hebrew was—and continues to be—a struggle for me. I have had to feel my way into its construction more than study my way in. As an adult learner, I knew I had reached a new plateau of growth when I heard and used a few Hebrew words I instantly understood, but couldn't really define in English. I was beginning to think as a Jew in Hebrew, which is to say, I was coming to understand what God wanted of me in my true native language—a kind of learning that went straight to my heart before it ever reached my brain.

Native Language

In language I am coming home now.
I did not know when I began
that shaping my lips around
these sounds would also shape my heart.
That soon, sooner than I knew for I did not
know at all . . .
the sounds would come from my heart before
they left my lips.

"And these words which I command you this day . . ."
I am not like the immigrant
desperate for the new language
that will guarantee survival
in an alien culture.

"shall be upon your heart . . ."
I have a permanent address
where almost every need is met
and yet I am a traveler still
in the country of my own blood.

"and you shall teach them diligently to your children . . ."
A visitor in my native land
I pay my gentle guides in a special currency of trust and work
to teach me the language that will let
me take the oath of citizenship.

"when you lie down and when you rise up . . ."
And so this morning when I read
Barukh atah Adonai Eloheinu melekh ha'olam, she'asani yisra'el
and understood it without thinking,

"in order that your days may be prolonged . . ."
I cried for knowing
that soon, sooner than I know
I will be in the place I want to be;

"and you will remember and fulfill all my commandments . . ."
speaking the native language of my soul,
crossing the border without a visa—

"and be holy unto your God."
a one-time tourist come home.

09/06/18

One uncharacteristically warm winter afternoon, I sat outside
reading a passage of Torah, an assignment in *Shemot* (Exodus) for
our women's study group. I was enjoying the weather, the work and
the quiet when the sun suddenly disappeared. Chilled, I glanced up
to gauge how long the interruption would last. I was shocked to see

that the sun was setting. Nearly three and a half hours had passed
while I, a person who feels undressed if I leave the house without
my watch, had sat studying Torah. I understood then that I hadn't
been studying at all. I had been visiting with God. On such visits,
who keeps track of the time?

Torah Study

My eyes scan the page for the familiar:
the shape of a letter, the presence of a root
whatever lets me know I am partly home—
able to utter a neural sigh of recognition.
"You I know."
"You I have seen before."
And I am hearing and seeing at once
even though I am only reading and thinking.
Rejoicing in my disorientation
I grope toward Jerusalem.
A willing player in an ancient
game of Blind Man's Bluff.
I think I am getting somewhere
until Torah takes over.
Barely understood concepts
play hide-and-seek with my brain.
I count to ten and shout my warning
but all the good ideas are already
hidden in the best places.
So I run as fast as my intellect will take me
searching even as I go
for the telltale signs of
passing.
The echo of phrase
the force of act
the sense of moment
the edge of symbol

the sweep of time
the thrust of word
the presence of God.
When I find the last
I cease to play.
Wild pleasure renders up full joy
as I forget where I end and God begins.
For a moment
we are both in the same place.
Studying Torah together.

The Joy of Learning or *Torah Lishmah*

Most startling of all was the unexpected conjunction between my
secular work as an independent school trustee and my religious
work as a Jewish learner. I knew a little bit about educational theory
from my years as a trustee at The Park School. As a Park School
alumna, I was the lucky beneficiary of an authentic progressive education. Most of all, I valued the cumulative effect of having had
dozens of teachers over the years who nourished my capacity to
think for myself, encouraged me to cultivate passions and taught me
to assess my performance against an internally monitored standard
of excellence, not an externally imposed one. I graduated from Park
at age seventeen with an abiding faith in the joy of learning—a sense
that learning is good for its sake alone. How stunning then as an
adult to discover that Judaism embraces the same principle! The
Rabbis in their long ago debates discovered what it took John Dewey
and a generation of his acolytes to articulate. What I thought Park
School had invented Judaism has known for centuries—learning is
life-giving. That is why we find joy in it; and that is why we do it. The
Jewish term for this principle is *Talmud Torah Lishmah,* "the study
of Torah for its own sake." It is what all adult learners who come to
Jewish learning of their own volition eventually experience, and it is
why we all find it—sooner or later—utterly irresistible.

The reason we love to learn is because we *need* to learn so we
can grow. I believe that the first story in Torah contains this

message. When God points out the Tree of Life and the Tree of Knowledge to Adam, God only forbids eating from the Tree of Knowledge. How fascinating that knowledge is represented in Torah as something man consumes, something for which he is endowed with an active appetite! And how amazing that, given the choice, man forgoes eternal life and chooses knowledge. To me, the Garden of Eden myth is most compelling as the story of man's introduction to consciousness. The Tree of Knowledge, *Aitz Hada'at tov v'rah,* is really much more than knowledge. The only other time the term *tov v'rah* occurs in Torah is in *Devarim* (Deuteronomy 1:39) where it is used to describe the children of the Israelites who were born after the Exodus and do not yet know *tov v'rah*—right from wrong. The inference is that children are not responsible for the mistakes their elders made, but they will be held accountable for their own actions once they are conscious and ready to take responsibility for *choosing* between right and wrong. A child is capable of this cognitive leap only when he is able to make a distinction between self and other, something that happens just about the same time he becomes verbal—what, in modern psychological terms, we call "self-consciousness." The singular recurrence of this phrase in Torah implies that for Adam and Eve partaking of the fruit of this tree signals a similar moment. They are born adult, presumably already in touch with the concept of self and other. Accordingly, their first recorded conversation, indicating the profound links between language, self consciousness and moral responsibility, takes place around their decision to eat the forbidden fruit.

Adam and Eve Were the First Adult Learners

Their very first insight after eating the fruit is the simultaneous realization that they are naked which leads to an immediate action—they clothe themselves. Although we have all been *taught* that they clothe themselves because they are ashamed, that is *not what the text says.* The text says that they clothe themselves because "the eyes of both of them were opened and they perceived that they were naked and they sewed together fig leaves and made themselves loinclothes" (Genesis 3:7). The very next feeling that is attributed to them as a result of their consciousness is not shame but *fear.* They hear God moving about and they hide because they are *afraid.* The sequence is straightforward. They eat the fruit, realize they are naked, cover themselves, then hide because they are afraid. The psychological parallel would be consciousness, vulnerability, defensiveness. There are two defensive responses: a physical one, covering with the fig leaf; and a behavioral one, hiding from God. How powerful this is as a paradigm for the new adult learner and for the place of Torah in Jewish life!

For all new adult learners of Judaism there is a similar moment when we suddenly acknowledge how ignorant we are of our own tradition. At that moment, we are incredibly vulnerable: On the verge of being able to receive wisdom, we are also so frightened that we might run away. But having the courage to admit our vulnerability allows a magnificent moment of self awareness that holds the potential for our adult Jewish liberation. We can stay as we are—ignorant and complacent. Or we can take responsibility for our deficiency, plunge into the world of Jewish learning, and begin to clothe ourselves in wisdom. Equally significant is what happens when we admit our deficiency and our need to *others.* Certainly God punished Adam and Eve for their disobedience, but God did a remarkable thing before sending them out of the garden. God gave them *better* clothing. God acknowledged their fear, vulnerability and real need and, in a supreme act of lovingkindness, gave them something more substantial than they could create for themselves.

The story of the Garden contains some extraordinary lessons. First, our appetite for knowledge is innate and divinely endowed, and fulfilling it satisfies us in a variety of ways. Second, acquiring knowledge is a dangerous business and has moral implications for which we are responsible. Third, self-consciousness is a precondition for receiving wisdom. We cannot discover what we need to know until we acknowledge what we do not know. Fourth, that moment of acknowledgment is fraught with psychological and physical tension: as human beings, we cannot tolerate our vulnerability for long before we have to *do* something about it. And fifth, awareness of our own mortality is the ultimate expression of consciousness.

Seeing the story in this way challenged me to reframe my own adult learning experience with a new set of questions: How seriously do we take the moment of acknowledgment for the new adult learner in our communities? Are we tuned in to it? Remembering where Adam and Eve's "moment" occurs, have we created environments safe and attractive enough to enable and "tempt" others to take similar risks? When they do take the risk and admit their vulnerability, how do we greet that admission—with disinterest, amusement, kindness, hostility or encouragement? Appreciating that we possess so many of the tools for the liberation of authentic Jewish learning, how prepared are we to share them? What range of programs and settings do we offer? How well do we understand the processes and challenges of adult learning? What kinds of curricula have we developed to address the specific cognitive and psychological sensibilities of the adult learner? How many teachers are truly competent in adult teaching? Do we have better wardrobe options than the first thing adult learners are most likely to grab—their inadequate baby blankets which have the sole advantage of comfort and familiarity?

It is no accident that the Rabbis refer to Torah as the Tree of Life. When we forfeited immortality in favor of consciousness, wisdom and the desire to learn, we chose another source of vitality for the continuing well-being of mankind—knowledge. If the source of all knowledge is Torah, then we chose Torah over immortality. Torah is what makes our lives worth living. Holding fast to Torah lets us achieve the only form of immortality available to us—the impact of our deeds and the legacy of our children. In Torah, we can find everything we need to live a rewarding life and all we need to know to teach our children.

Authentic Learning Takes Many Forms

I have had many rewards as an adult learner because I have had the incredibly good fortune to belong to a congregation that takes adult learning seriously. I have had demanding teachers with high expectations and exacting standards. I've learned with some of our country's great scholars and been encouraged to find ways to use what I've learned to teach others. Likewise, I have been encouraged to learn some things for no other reason than that they would be meaningful to me. I learned how to chant *"Shirat Ha'yam,"* the Song of the Sea, sung by the Israelites after they pass safely through the Reed Sea, because I believed from my studies that the song had a special power and meaning for women. I thought that learning to chant it would brand me, a comfortable, safe American Jew, and sear in the experience–the terror and the euphoria–of the Exodus. I wanted to sing for Miriam, the leader of the professional women's chorus that in ancient times was comprised of virgins and women past child-bearing age, and designated to chant on behalf of the community in times of sorrow and triumph. Knowing that women played this specific public role in the ritual life of ancient Israel, it made sense to me to think of *"Shirat Ha'yam"* as Miriam's song. The day that I stood on the *bimah* and chanted that epic piece was the first time that I felt like a full participant in the ritual life of *my* congregation. And I was as close to God in public as I had ever been. Torah and the moment allowed me to chant myself straight into a divine space, a sacred dimension where time was shattered into a thousand insignificant pieces. I was simply an instrument then–giving voice to God's words–and the sound was all that mattered. In reclaiming an ancient Jewish female role, I reclaimed a part of myself. Chanting it wasn't an act of defiant feminist triumphalism; it was more like taking a lost object back to its rightful owner. Once I had found it, I was obliged to try to return it.

There were other lessons to be learned as long as I remained open to their possibility. Following the firm advice of a young rabbi impatient with my complaint about the difficulty of mastering prayers in Hebrew–"Just study for fifteen minutes a day then. There's no excuse for not being able to do *that*"–I spent an entire summer learning the daily *Amidah*. There was no goal except to learn the *Amidah*–but it stunned me that it took that long to gain fluency. I studied over a congregational resident scholar weekend with Dr. Peter Pitzele, a member of the Jewish Theological Seminary faculty. A pioneer in the creation of bibliodrama, he showed us how the application of specific dramatic techniques could "crack open" biblical texts. I could barely control my excitement. His teaching unlocked familiar texts in provocative new ways and provided me with an interpretive tool that I could immediately begin to use. While I wrote the women's study group *midrash* on Sarah as a self-imposed exercise, I soon realized that I couldn't take full credit for the end result. Something far more profound than study was happening. Again, I had entered a sacred realm, not only the encounter with the text but the encounter with our tradition. Consciously and unconsciously, I found myself working with intricate literary patterns and fundamental theological questions. I began to appreciate a unique characteristic of sacred texts: they automatically elicit rhythms and repetitions—even unintentional ones. They call upon higher powers than we know we possess.

I have also discovered that authentic Jewish learning can occur anywhere if done in the proper spirit. My involvement in the Institute for Christian-Jewish Studies, a Baltimore organization that fosters transformative interfaith dialogue through deep text-based study, has helped me advance my understanding of my own sacred texts as well as those of Christianity and to appreciate that ignorance of either is crippling. I can't aspire to any kind of adult competence without a working knowledge of the two foundational texts of western life. Furthermore, I can, in the presence of thoughtful, enlightened Christians, drop the tiresome fears inbred by centuries of anti-Semitism and begin to explore the positive lessons of Christianity. I no longer need to approach Christianity as the oppressive lens through which I view my Jewish identity—a struggling specimen pinned to the viewing platform of a microscope. Instead, I can call upon a more dynamic model that permits me to explore how the two traditions have historically borrowed from and engaged with one another. We are truly connected—two lenses of one telescope aimed at God. Christianity is no longer the "other" whose greatest value to me is as a counterpoint. Instead, my sense of who I am as a Jew has been expanded by better understanding what it means to be a Christian, since the two faiths continue to evolve and have much to teach one another.

Likewise, traveling to Israel on three different community study missions and seeing the country through non-Jewish eyes extended *my* Israeli vision. Spared the overt sentimentality and contrivances of most Federation missions, I was finally able to admit that the Western Wall more alienated than moved me while the sight of Israeli schoolchildren with military escorts staggered me. That Yad Vashem simply made me angry while Yemin Orde, an extraordinary orphans' community, restored my faith in the country and its purpose.

Throughout all of my learning runs a constant tension between learning to do and doing to learn. I need both in order to grow. Perhaps most importantly, doing and learning in a congregation where doctors, lawyers, carpenters, secretaries, stay-at-home moms and retired people are actively engaged in both activities tells all of us that this is critical, exciting and life-affirming work. We need it for ourselves and we need it for our community. We learn and study because we need to understand the divine truths that underlie creation and our lives and to discover what God's will for us is. Learning becomes essential when we determine that the *only* way our lives will have meaning is if they are an expression of a transcendent moral order and not a random set of guidelines which we abide by when— and if—the spirit moves us. When we stop learning, we stop growing. When we stop growing, we die. Learning, as our sages understood, and as I have experienced, is life itself. To learn and grow as an adult is a blessing and a privilege I hope never to take for granted and always to enjoy.

7

It's Fine for You, but
What About the Rest of Us?

*There are three crowns: the crown of Torah, the crown of
Priesthood, the crown of royalty. The crown of a good name is
superior to them all.*

—Pirke Avot IV:17

The truth is that I needed an additional impetus to get me moving
down this path and to keep me on it once I started. It was the image
of myself as a flawed and ignorant Jewish leader that first made me
gauge the depth and breadth of my Jewish identity. It was my role as
a philanthropist that gave me the tools to try do something about the
"continuity problem" and to appreciate how bankrupt my philanthropy would be if what I proposed was crucial for others but not
necessary for me. The combined roles gave me remarkable opportunities to travel around the country meeting other Jewish leaders and
philanthropists and learning that many of us had similar experiences.
Looking back, I doubt that I could have sustained the energy and
focus of these past four years without the added incentive of becoming a more knowledgeable Jewish leader and philanthropist. And I
suffer no illusions that I often benefited from a special kind of attention *because* I am a leader and a philanthropist.

Some cynics may conclude that only people with access to
power and money can achieve a similar growth. They might ask
themselves, "Now if *I*, your average Jew, suddenly decided at age
forty-something that I wanted to explore my Judaism, would my
rabbi take an interest in me the way Hendler's has with her? Would

I get private Torah lessons from the director of *Melitz* (which provides Judaic religious curricula for Israeli schools) whenever he
came to town? Would my Federation's senior educational officer
study *Pirke Avot* and the *Chagim* (the Jewish holidays) with me?
Would a rabbi at the local yeshiva ask me if I would like to be his student? Could *I* go on my synagogue board and be president five years
later?"

I've yet to encounter an "average Jew," so I'm not quite sure
what the term means. But the challenge from these questions is legitimate since they get to the heart of the matter for every adult
learner and seeker. The real question is: "If I am serious about this,
will anybody pay attention to me?" My answer is yes. There isn't a
dedicated rabbi in this country who wouldn't be thrilled to help any
congregant who was earnest about pursuing their growth as a Jew.
Some may not know how to help—a failing of their training more
than a reflection of their concern—but most will eagerly support the
genuine learner. No, Avram Infeld, *Melitz*'s director, probably
wouldn't give you a private lesson because you wouldn't be meeting
with him to sustain a long-term family funding relationship. On the
other hand, if you were like most funders, he wouldn't be teaching
you much Torah, either. You would certainly be free, however, to
attend the public lessons he gives during his visits to the United
States. And it is unlikely that a senior Federation officer would offer
to study with you out of the blue, but if he was the educational con-
sultant to a model program you were trying to launch and saw you
avidly pursuing your own Jewish education, he might propose studying together.

And the yeshiva? The Orthodox are the most experienced of all
our denominations at targeted, deliberate outreach. They are dedicated to creating new adherents on a one-to-one basis, patiently
building up the Jewish people one Jew at a time. They will help anyone, anywhere, anytime who is serious about Jewish learning. They
might have the *chutzpah* to seek you out if you have some stature
and means in the community, but you could have the *chutzpah* to
contact them for learning and they would definitely respond.

And the synagogue? Who I am definitely influenced the decision
to invite me onto the fast track of synagogue leadership. But more

important, I hope, was my record of achievement. After eighteen years as a non-profit volunteer, my experience included chairmanships, fundraising responsibilities, long-range planning and fiscal management skills. In truth, I wish more people with these skills were beating down the doors to synagogues. I hope that a decade from now they will be. I know that when I was given the opportunity to serve my synagogue, I leapt at it—grateful for the chance to be useful, eager to give something back to the place that was so deeply and profoundly influencing my life. I also know that if I had entered into any of these learning or leadership relationships believing that I was entitled to be in them by virtue of privilege alone, or that the only reason others sought me out was access to the power they imagined I represent, no worthy learning or leadership could have taken place. The relationships would have been contaminated from the start.

Growing up Jewish in America could make you a little schizoid, but growing up wealthy and Jewish in America could make you paranoid. Some wealthy Jews are convinced that their money is the *only* reason others seek relationships with them. Unfortunately, they're right—in the way of all self-fulfilling prophecies. If that's all they expect from others, that's all that they'll receive. More than a few of them can recount truly sad stories of dysfunctional families of their own, and of parents substituting privileges and material goods for personal attention and love. I know that for many of them, inheriting wealth they didn't earn places a painful burden on their shoulders. Some shrink from the weight of it; some are permanently infantilized by it; some are unable to live the lives they want to live, constantly vulnerable to the charge that whatever they accomplish or achieve is mostly due to preferential treatment—and rarely due to their own merit.

Growing Up with Lucy and Ricky

Fortunately, my parents did not raise me or my siblings to live that way. They had a clear philosophy of child-rearing, they were absolutely comfortable with their growing wealth and power, and they had a deep conviction that they were raising kids who would all be leaders. The idea of raising philanthropists only occurred later when we were all young adults and the sale of our publicly-owned business made the establishment of additional foundations (apart from the one initially created by my grandfather) possible. Like most children who admire and love their parents, I turned out in many ways to be exactly the person they intended me to be: I am doing work they would approve of in a way they would respect.

Identities are first formed in families and the relationship that most deeply influences a child's view of the world and herself is the relationship she sees between her parents. Like many families, a certain mythology surrounded my parents' relationship with each other. As a child, I thought that husbands and wives who love each other never argue. I was stunned whenever I witnessed parental squabbles in other people's homes. It was obvious that my mother absolutely delighted my father. Thumbing her nose at convention was a lifelong hobby for Mom—one she embraced with style and verve. Sometimes, at parties, she would drop to the floor in full evening dress and challenge the male guests to a one-armed push-up contest. She dove off the high dive at a local country club when she was five months pregnant with me, at a time when women still hid their bellies behind voluminous tent dresses. She once started a stampede of a local farmer's dairy herd by honking a specialty horn she'd installed in our van; "Look, kids," she said, "you wanna see something funny?" She regularly challenged authority of all kinds, sometimes appropriately and sometimes not. At one level, she lived her entire life in rebellion; at another level, she was teaching us valuable lessons about the dangers of complacency and the lazy comfort that familiarity, privilege and safety can breed.

My father got such a kick out of her! Their relationship had a rhythm and comic purity that elicited amusement and admiration from all who observed them together. Mom was Lucy Ricardo with money and Dad was Ricky with influence and an American accent. He thrived on her outrageous behavior, her incredibly down-to-earth sense of humor that deflated pomposity and arrogance, her contagious energy and vitality. We all did. We relied on her to spice things up when the predictability and domesticity of our comfortable lives threatened to dull our senses or our appreciation of life. She could shake us out of our lethargy in an instant, sometimes by simply declaring a sudden need for an interesting story at the dinner table. She would greet with equal enthusiasm an account of a spelling bee victory or the loss of a playground brawl. During our recitations of school tribulations and triumphs, Dad displayed his wide-ranging knowledge. From history to English to French to science to math, he knew a little bit about everything that we were learning. Just enough to ask penetrating questions and to challenge us when we gave him superficial answers.

Dad taught us practical skills while Mom urged us to take physical, emotional and psychological risks. When we were very little, Mom would perch us in trees—and walk away. If we whined, she'd tell us to stop complaining and figure out how to get out of the tree if we wanted to get down so badly. Soon, we were tree monkeys. She threw us into the water for our first swim lessons. She was ready to leap in if need be, but she knew it wouldn't be necessary. When we complained that we were bored because we didn't live in a neighborhood with ready-made friends, she'd respond without an ounce of compassion in her voice, "Well that's not *my* problem now is it? Go figure it out for yourselves." Dad showed us how to build things, how to catch and throw a ball properly, make a campfire and fix a broken toilet. Through all of this, we learned to think that whatever the challenge, "*I* can do that." And whatever the threat, "*I* can handle that."

Now I understand that my parents were deliberately breeding independence, resourcefulness and resilience into us. They were teaching us to have faith in ourselves and to regularly test that faith. They were practicing a form of American Zionism, and were as determined as the early modern settlers of Israel to fashion a new breed of Jew. They emphatically rejected the image of the Jew as victim and disdained the stereotype of the eastern European Jew so painfully captured in Hayyim Nachman Bialik's classic 1904 poem, "The City of Slaughter." That poem, which every Israeli schoolchild can recite, proclaimed that Jewish exile and punishment were not the result of sin, but the political consequence of rearing weak, passive men who cowered and prayed in vain while their wives, daughters, mothers and sisters were being brutally raped and slaughtered. Bialik's radical interpretation of the Kishnev Pogrom rallied early Zionists around a singular vision of the Jew as strong and capable repossessor of the land.

Completely independent of the Jewish drama playing out halfway across the world, but coming to similar conclusions in the aftermath of the Holocaust, my parents were writing their own script for Jewish empowerment. Calling upon her Midwestern reverence for farming, Mom moved us from the manicured and constrained world of the Jewish neighborhood ghetto to the wide-open world of Christian rural expanses. She drove a huge Ford farm tractor, and used it to mow the lower half of our fourteen-acre property. She loved animals and taught us to love them. Over the years, our menagerie included chickens, ponies, goats, sheep, a raccoon, a woolly monkey and countless dogs and cats (and those were only the animals we kept outside). I didn't know any other Jewish mothers (much less Jewish fathers) who drove farm tractors, could tame a wild raccoon or thought that women should have muscles. Physicality and closeness to the land were essential ingredients in the formula my parents were using to raise us. They divined in these sources a special nourishment for our future success. Without them, we might become another generation of pasty-faced Jews doomed to play out the shameful Diaspora drama of victimized wanderer.

My parents' leadership development curriculum contained other lessons as well. Mom and Dad had the unusual wisdom to refrain from using their power and influence to protect us from life's nastier lessons. They understood that loving us was *allowing* us to get hurt. So they stood back, letting us clean up our own messes and earn our own bruises and scars. And they taught us about discipline—not the Jewish discipline necessary to the pursuit of holiness, but the secular discipline requisite for the pursuit of excellence. Dad's favorite child-rearing axiom was, "If you're going to do something, do it right." This expectation applied not only to our homework and extracurricular activities, but extended to floor-sweeping, bed-making, car-cleaning—any menial task a kid would like to finish as quickly as possible so she could get to more important things like tree-climbing or bike-riding. Of course, our plans were no match for Dad's determination. We were regularly summoned out of trees and off bikes to do the chore all over again and "do it right" under his exacting supervision.

Obsessed with our handshakes, Mom drilled us over and over again on the firmness of our grip and the direct eye contact a memorable greeting requires. When we were in restaurants, she made us cross the room to introduce ourselves to adults she knew but whom we had never met. She considered self-introduction a necessary skill and she was right, although I hated the lesson because of the four children in our family, I was the shy one. My parents were preparing us for the public roles they believed each of us would eventually play. So they taught us to handle ourselves with courtesy and integrity around powerful people: No fawning, no gushing. We met governors, mayors and members of Congress. We sat at the "family table" in huge banquet halls at events honoring our grandparents or parents, and learned to acknowledge the attention we received without feeling self-conscious or diminished. Being "on display" was part of belonging to an influential family.

Our "training" took place without a single lecture or explanation. We were expected to draw our own conclusions. Some conclusions, however, were not left to chance. While Mom could, through sheer force of personality, enter a room and take it over, Dad did it only when he had the authority to do so. He was acutely aware of the effect of his power on those around him and the tremendous responsibility that power carried, not solely in terms of the good it could do but the harm it might cause as well. And Dad had a genuine reverence for the middle class of this country which, he maintained, had made the nation great. He believed the average middle-class American was overlooked, undervalued and often mistreated. I never heard him use a different tone of voice for a different "class" of individual. He spoke with the same patience, respect and care to the gardener, the cook and the job foreman as he did to the chairman of the board, the chief of staff and the governor.

The moment that hammered this lesson home more than any other was one of the few times I ever recall seeing my father lose his temper.

Jill, Joe and I were riding with my father in his car one weekday past a public high school that was letting out for the afternoon. Suddenly, Jill sneered, "Oh, look at all those hicks!" Dad hit the brakes and pulled the car off to the side of the road.

"What did you say?" he yelled.

Jill giggled a little because his reaction was so uncharacteristic she thought he was joking. "I *said* 'Look at all those hicks.' They *are*, you know. Hicks, I mean." She scrambled to cover her tracks once she realized she'd made a mistake.

Dad turned fully around in his seat to fix both of us with a glare of enormous disappointment and rage. "Just who the hell do you think you are?" he roared. "Do you think you're better than them because you go to private school? Do you think you're *special* just because you happen to live in this family? I've got news for you. You're no better. You're just luckier. You have no right to make fun of someone else because they aren't as fortunate as you are or because you're getting a private education and live in a nicer house. 'There but for the grace of God go I.' I will never ever hear that kind of language from *any* of my children again! Do you understand?"

"Yes, Daddy," we whispered in unison.

"Good," he answered abruptly, "and don't you *ever* forget it."

Together, Mom and Dad worked out the delicate choreography of distinction, teaching us the sometimes subtle, sometimes obvious differences between privilege and entitlement, obligation and burden, authority and arrogance, wealth and profligacy, power and corruption. Through all of this ran the unmistakable strand of expectation: We *would* learn these lessons. And we *would* live our lives based on them.

Wealth and Power Don't Have to Corrupt

The most ironic feature of Jewish ambivalence about power, wealth, inheritance and true accomplishment is that our tradition has lots to say on the subject. Unfortunately, few of us have spent enough time studying Torah to even know that it contains stories on these issues. We seem to believe that wealth inherently corrupts, yet our patriarchs were wealthy guys by anyone's standards. Jacob's shrewdness as a shepherd was legendary. Isaac, the only patriarch to stay home, inherited Abraham's wealth, but ultimately demonstrated his own diplomatic and business acumen. He avoided strife, dug wells and improved on his inheritance to the point of making his neighbors envious. Abraham, who basically started out with nothing like so many of our immigrant forefathers, built himself a sizeable estate. Judaism has no sentimental notions about a special salvation that the economically disadvantaged may expect. Our Rabbis teach that if all the ills of the world were put on one side of a scale and poverty on the other, poverty would outweigh them all. Living in poverty, they seem to be saying, cuts deeper than simply making it difficult to meet our everyday needs of food, shelter and clothing. Poverty afflicts the spirit. Indeed, its presence jeopardizes our very humanity. And impoverishment in this world doesn't entitle us to special consideration in the world to come. On the other hand, no particular entitlement is attached to being rich, either. In fact, we are cautioned over and over again in matters of justice to guard against currying favor with the rich (for possible current or future gain) or pandering to the poor (out of a misguided sentimental sympathy). A magnificent morning prayer, adapted from Leviticus, captures this beautifully: "Do not be partial to the poor or show deference to the rich; judge your neighbor fairly. . . ." What our tradition is suggesting is that each person must be judged on his or her own merit, not on the expectations and assumptions we assign to an individual based on what we know or think we know about them because of their station in life. The evidence on which we judge our fellow human beings must be the evidence we *see,* not the evidence we imagine.

Because money wasn't an issue for my parents, it was seldom an issue for us. Without guilt or confusion, they taught us to enjoy the wonderful things money can buy: nice clothes, exciting trips, private education, fabulous summer opportunities, a gracious home. It would be disingenuous to suggest my parents taught us thrift, but they certainly taught us not to be spendthrifts. An implicit rule guided all of our purchasing choices: There was a difference between an appropriate expenditure and an inexcusable indulgence that reflected a lack of social responsibility and good sense—and we were expected to know that difference. Most importantly, we saw our parents and grandparents eagerly respond to the many opportunities they were given to serve their community. It was obvious that service and leadership gave their lives additional purpose and meaning. As we grew older, I saw my father's pile of nightly business work gradually transform into a pile of communal work. He took delight in transferring his for-profit skills to the non-profit arena. And Mom was indefatigable, championing her latest project with the same devotion she had lavished on the one before. She took on projects the way other people went on shopping sprees.

The sale of our real estate business in 1979 ushered in a new era of opportunity for our family's leadership and philanthropy. Not only did my parents use the sale to set up foundations in their own name, they also used it to create a philanthropic fund to be run solely by their four children who ranged in age, at the time, from nineteen to twenty-nine. A radical innovation when set up almost two decades ago, the Children of Harvey and Lyn Meyerhoff Philanthropic Fund (our choice of name, not my parents') was designed to prepare us to manage major future philanthropic responsibilities. The first rule we established was nonnegotiable: we agreed that we could not use the fund our parents had established to fulfill our own communal obligations. Nothing prepared us better for the demands of responsible philanthropy than the sobering pleasure of signing checks drawn on our own accounts. And nothing delighted our parents more than knowing that we arrived at this conclusion entirely on our own.

It was my experience with the fund, in fact, that springboarded me into my role as a national speaker on philanthropy. In the early fall of 1993, Darrell Friedman, the executive vice president of Baltimore's Federation, asked me to participate in a plenary session at the General Assembly (GA), the Council of Jewish Federations' (CJF's) annual conference for North American Jewish Federation leaders. The proposed program would feature a senior philanthropist and me addressing the new "hot button" issue of "intergenerational philanthropy." I thought about it for a few days and called Darrell to decline the invitation, convinced that what the CJF wanted me to say and what I felt compelled to say were irreconcilable. I couldn't compliment the expected audience on a job magnificently done since I believed that many of them were missing the boat. They hadn't raised children who cared as passionately about Jewish life as they did and now they expected their money to do what their child-rearing had failed to achieve. There was too much money at stake for CJF to risk offending their most generous donors with the kind of speech I wanted to give.

Darrell refused to accept my "regrets." "Lee," he cajoled, "I need you to *do* this. We have to start getting this message out, changing the way we do business. We think you're the right person, believe me. You can do it without offending them. You respect these people. And that makes all the difference."

"Oh God," I responded, "this is my 'coming out' party!"

We laughed because it was true. But we also realized that this was a pivotal moment for me. I was being given a remarkable opportunity to integrate my personal journey with my public work in a national forum. What I did with it was up to me. I was stunned when ten days before the GA, Darrell called to tell me that the senior leader who was scheduled to speak before me had backed out. After a soul-searching review of his own track record, he determined he had nothing to say. None of his kids were involved in the ways he had hoped; none shared his convictions. He considered himself a failure in intergenerational philanthropy. This dramatically reinforced what I already knew. Most of us were doing poorly in this new endeavor, and it was my job to explain why I thought this was the case and to propose some possible solutions.

The day after my speech, the phone rang early. Darrell's voice came soaring out of the receiver. "Lee?"

"You were expecting someone else at 7:00 in the morning?"

"Are you sitting or standing?"

"I'm lounging in bed with my first box of bonbons. I'm running around the kitchen trying to get the kids off to school!"

"Sit down for a minute, Lee. You won't believe what's going on here. People are passing around copies of your speech. One man stood up at the end of a plenary session yesterday, said that he had

been coming to GA's for twenty-five years and had just heard the
best speech of his life. This is big, Lee. Very big. Professionals have
been asking if you'll come to their communities. You're an overnight
sensation. You mother would be so proud of you!"

Darrell was right—Mom would have been proud if a little puzzled
at my message of deliberately integrating Judaism into our lives in a
way that could directly infuse and influence our philanthropy. I
could just hear her: "What do you *think* we're doing when we fund
Jewish causes, helping out the Catholic Church?" In characteristic
fashion, Dad had passed me a note in the middle of my speech. I
missed a beat and opened it: "SLOW DOWN." For a split second, I
felt like Alice reading, "DRINK ME." Still giving me instructions even
though I was forty-one. He was thrilled when it was all over. How
strange that making your parents proud at forty-one could still mean
as much as when you were ten.

My parents' concept of leadership reflected their own life experience: the searing events of the Holocaust and the birth of the State
of Israel; their coming of age on the eve of World War II and their
deeply inbred patriotism; their driving ambition to succeed as Americans—undeterred by others' prejudices—on American terms in ways
their immigrant forefathers could only dream of. For them, philanthropy and *tzedakah* were synonymous. They had convictions and
the will and the money to see them through. They also understood
money in a distinctly Jewish way: They used it, enjoyed it, and refused to romanticize or idealize it. They saw it as a tool to redress in-
justice, one more way to help make the world a slightly better place
than when they found it. And as leaders they found many good ways
to use their money. My father was the first Jewish president of the
Johns Hopkins Health Systems, and the first Jew to chair the central
Maryland United Way campaign. My mother was a driving force behind establishing the popular National Aquarium in Baltimore, the
catalyst for the first full-service digestive disease center in North
America, a delegate to the United Nations, and one of the first people to articulate a distinctly American rationale for the United States
Holocaust Memorial Museum. My father committed himself to my
mother's deathbed wish to make sure that the Museum was built and
spent six years as its chairman making good on that promise.

Although Jewish causes always had the first call on their dollar, being Americans is what fired their imaginations and captured their hearts. What *I* have been free to choose is the degree to which Judaism influences the work I undertake and the way I execute my philanthropic and leadership responsibilities. I want to see the world—and the work I am privileged to do—through a distinctly and explicitly Jewish lens. Now I have a much clearer notion of what that means—and of all I want it to mean. And I've learned that all Jewish leaders should be Jewish learners. We can look to Moses or King David as our model or to any of the other great matriarchs and patriarchs around whom rabbinic tradition has created *midrashim* related to learning. It is apocryphal, of course, to read that Isaac went to yeshiva when he departed from Abraham after the thwarted sacrifice at Mount Moriah, or to read that Jacob stayed in his tent and out of the fields as a boy because he was studying Torah. Torah hadn't yet been given to the Jewish people! The point is more profound than the niggling issue of historical accuracy. Our sages are saying that authentic Jewish leaders must be learned Jews, fluent in our tradition, and conversant with our sacred texts. Jewish learning and Jewish leadership go hand in hand. Somewhere along the line we stopped insisting on that handshake, and relegated learning to others to safeguard while our leaders got on with the business of leadership. I know now that I cannot be the kind of leader that I want to be unless I am a learning Jew. I have to be "bilingual"—fluent in Judaism and equally conversant in secular skills. When I am a learning Jew in the presence of other learning Jews, I am rediscovering my purpose and God's intention all over again. I am no more important—and no less important—than my fellow students. Learning is the great equalizer in Jewish life and Torah is the instrument of equalization because we are all equally important before God. The only requirement for participation is seriousness. Anyone who is serious will receive the attention they need regardless of who they are.

But leadership is more complicated. The universal equalizer *should* be performance, but other factors count, as well. If the non-profit world let its members elect their leaders, I would be an unlikely candidate in most instances. Selected leaders are different from elected leaders. I know I have been selected, not elected, for every position I currently hold and that no sweeping mandate has ever carried me into any office. Our lives *do* get contaminated by power and privilege and the natural differences that the luck of the genetic draw and circumstances dictate. Some of us do have more opportunities than others. Some of us are graced with more gifts but we *all* have gifts and opportunities. What really matters is what we make of what we've got. In that way—and that way alone—we all truly start from the same place. We are all leaders of one kind or another. Sometime, somewhere, somehow—during each of our lives—another human being will look to us for guidance, direction or example. How each of us responds to that challenge is our "moment" of leadership.

I hope to be judged by what I did with those moments during my lifetime: by what I've achieved, not by what people choose to assume about me. This is how Judaism tells us we ought to judge one another—by act, not intention or assumption. The world would be a different place, indeed, if we all believed that, as *Pirke Avot* says, "There are three crowns: the crown of Torah, the crown of Priesthood, the crown of royalty. The crown of a good name is superior to them all." I would love to live in such a world. Until we get there, however, I can only behave as if we do.

8

You're Not Putting That Thing on Our Lawn!

Also you shall not oppress the stranger for you know the heart of the stranger: seeing as you were strangers in the land of Egypt.
—Exodus 23:9

This is the chapter I almost left out. I worried that providing a laundry list of all the difficulties my family has experienced might furnish more excuses than we—and our culture—already provide for avoiding a serious exploration of Judaism. But the alternative seemed worse. I didn't want to leave the reader with the misguided impression that the kind of personal transformation I've undergone could occur in a vacuum. When one person in a family undergoes a radical change, *everyone* is affected. If the process is real, there is no way to avoid repercussions. And a truthful account should not whitewash the effect of those repercussions.

The truth is that when we walk freely, of our own accord, toward Judaism, we often make ourselves into strangers, and "the community" is not yet prepared to give us the kind of support we need. The marriage ceremony is a helpful metaphor for explaining what I mean. On one side of the aisle sits our family, the people we know and love, the family we are in some way leaving. On the other side sits the family we are in some way joining, people we imagine we will come to know and love. But we walk down the aisle without an escort. No one stands at our elbow whispering encouraging words of either love or instruction. The relationship we are moving toward is with God and the people Israel, so no visible groom awaits us under the *chuppah,* the marriage canopy. Everyone is gathered to witness, but only *we* can take responsibility for what happens. We hope everyone wishes us well, but we know that many do not. The family we are leaving is often angry because they haven't been consulted and didn't authorize what we have chosen to do. They are frightened that we will become a stranger to them. The family we are joining isn't rushing to greet us with open arms because they have no idea who or what we are. They're not so sure about this stranger in their midst. *We* made the decision to join *them,* not the other way around. So for a while, we aren't truly welcome in the new community we are entering or fully welcome in the home we have not really left. Instead, we end up shuttling back and forth between the two sides of the aisle—trying to please everyone—as we struggle to piece together our new identity without putting all the relationships we cherish at risk. Or we walk quietly down the middle with as much dignity as we can muster, hoping that everyone on both sides will eventually figure out a way to love us as much as we love them.

None of this is much of a problem, of course, if husband, wife and kids are of one accord. I've watched several families undertake the process of becoming more serious about Judaism together. It is nothing like what I've experienced. They have a shared vision of destination. Although genuine transformation is never *easy,* these families are impressive to watch for they do not have to absorb the shock and disorientation of "strangerhood" that Torah warns us about. Even when they are strangers in the community (and they always are for a period of time) they are never strangers to each other in their own home. They always have a refuge from strangerhood. I admire them from afar and occasionally I even envy them. Mostly, though, I am delighted by them, because they are going forward with the blessing of the people they most love in the world. It is remarkable to encounter Judaism this way, and I hope they appreciate how fortunate they are. Unfortunately for *me,* I'm not one of them, but I believe my experience more closely approximates that of a whole other group of adult Jews. For now, *we* are the larger group, and if the American Jewish community is serious about reinventing itself, it must pay closer attention to us.

Unshared transformation requires patience, a thick skin, a sense of humor, a good memory, love and empathy. I have not always had all those qualities in abundance and do not claim to have them now, but during the last four years, I've developed a heightened awareness of their value and necessity. Although I remain confused by the resistance, the scorn and even the anger I have encountered, especially in my own family, I am committed to trying to understand it. It's easier to deal with a problem we understand since instinct and resolve can take us only so far.

While studying Jewish leaders in a community in the South, an ethnographer I know made an unexpected discovery: a number of them were becoming serious Jewish learners. She had come upon one disturbing finding, however, when she returned to the community for a follow-up visit. Four of the women who had seen themselves as "happily married" at the beginning of their Jewish journeys were now considering divorce. I was not surprised. When we discussed Shabbat and *kashrut* in our study group and three or four women grew teary-eyed as they confessed their fears of alienating their families if they "went too far," I knew exactly what they were talking about. I also knew what it cost them to live with their pain. Getting serious about Judaism in many Jewish families is the equivalent of becoming a deserter or traitor. What many adult seekers find so attractive about Judaism—the opportunity to incorporate belief into systematic daily behavior and to place home and family at the center of our new belief system—can often place us at direct cross-purposes with our families. If we want to reduce the conflict that arises, then we must learn to better anticipate and plan for its inevitability. I *did* expect resistance from my family, but I never imagined it would be as deep-seated and emotional as it often turned out to be.

The Mother's Day from Hell

I knew the very first day I went to synagogue that I had taken an irreversible step away from my husband and kids and that I, not they, would have to bear the brunt of responsibility for that decision. After all, it was *my* choice, not theirs. I didn't ask their permission. I knew better. If I had, it's unlikely it would ever have been granted. Likewise, I didn't expect them to join me. What I didn't imagine is that they would try so hard to undermine and challenge the choices I did make.

Apart from insisting on a better Jewish education for my children, I did not demand anything else of my family. I knew that my own changing behavior and beliefs did not entitle me to impose them on others. Insisting on their active support and participation might have permanently damaged our relationships. The resulting trauma would be indefensible, especially in light of what Judaism teaches us: apart from God, there is no more important relationship than the one we have with our families. Exercising restraint and respect for who my family was meant that I almost always had to make more compromises than they did. In some way, the process had a salutary effect on me. It slowed me down and made me more conscious of every choice I made because there were two parties to take into account with every decision—me and my family. So I observe as much of *kashrut*, the Jewish dietary laws, as I can without insisting that we keep a kosher home (which, of course, means that I can't *really* observe *kashrut*). Though I go to synagogue every Saturday morning, I don't make my children go. Though I don't shop on Shabbat, it doesn't mean that they can't. Though I won't drive anywhere for myself other than to *shul* on Shabbat, it doesn't mean that they can't go to art class and that I won't pick them up. Everyone who is in town is expected to be home for Shabbat dinner on Friday night, but even that requirement has been waived on occasion. The problem runs deeper than any inconveniences my newfound devotion creates. If that were all that was involved, we would have resolved the resentments a long time ago through straightforward negotiation. But how do we negotiate feelings? How do we counteract the confusion and resentment that repudiation creates?

At almost every juncture, my turning *toward* something I valued was interpreted as a turning *away* from something they valued. One of the great temptations for someone who has just discovered the possibility and power of religion is to behave as if she were the newly appointed arbiter of proper religious conduct. I've tried to guard against this tendency and I've been disappointed when a certain tone creeps into my voice: a school teacher delivering doctrine, a seeker of faith condescending to speak to the heathens. I can play this role convincingly and I know that it is not attractive or endearing. I wince, for example, as I remember my reaction when I blessed my children at Shabbat dinner in my sister's home and she asked, "Why do you do that?"

It was just the invitation I needed to tell everyone more than they ever wanted to know about the ritual, and Jewish parenthood and theology. Too late, I recalled the warning from a good friend, "Telling is not teaching, Lee." I lost my audience three minutes into the explanation. Of course, I sulked for twenty minutes afterwards because my lecture ended abruptly with my nephew's imitation of a newscaster, "Uh, thanks for the update, Aunt Lee. That oughta 'bout wrap it up, don't you think? Who cares? Let's eat!" Everyone laughed, but I was stunned and hurt. I should have asked my sister what *she* thought it meant. I should have bided my time and suggested we discuss it over dinner instead of while everyone was waiting to attack the buffet. I should have, but I didn't. And they should have been kinder, but they weren't.

And I remember the first night *seder* a few years ago when a difficult question arose. Someone chirped, "Ask the rabbi!" and everyone turned to me. The problem was that the speaker's teasing lilt also had a darker note of antipathy and derision. In three words, the speaker conveyed my family's discomfort and deep ambivalence about the way I had broken ranks by choosing to become a learned Jew.

In the spring of 1994, after a great deal of thought, I announced to Nelson and the kids that I was going to begin observing *kashrut*. I talked with them about becoming aware of God every time I ate and committing myself to a discipline that would raise my consciousness of holiness and my potential to achieve it. But my family wasn't really interested in my reasons as long as they could still eat cheeseburgers. The real sacrifice for me was giving up shellfish. Food seldom excites me but I could always work up an appetite for a pile of freshly steamed crabs or a bucket of clams. So I was a little taken aback when, two weeks after my announcement, Nelson declared that we were going to go to a local crabhouse for Mother's Day. The double irony was striking. Not only was he going to test me, but the occasion for the test was supposed to be my reward for being a good Mommy.

"Don't you remember, honey?" I protested softly. "I said I wouldn't be eating shellfish anymore. I want to keep kosher."

"Oh, come on. Stop being such a stick-in-the-mud. It'll be fun. You can start tomorrow. It's Mother's Day. Loosen up!"

I was loosened up enough to want to haul off and clout him. "Don't you think it would be nice to go someplace where I could eat?"

"You can eat there. If you're really not going to have any crabs, you can order fish."

"I *don't* want to go there, Nel. Please."

"I've already made reservations and told the kids."

This was beginning to look more sinister than an insensitive, spontaneous suggestion. It was a shoot-out at high noon. First one to blink bit the dust. I realized that if I didn't go, Nelson would win in some weird way even though I was "right." So I climbed into the car and rode off to the Mother's Day dinner that I wouldn't—and couldn't—eat. The kids, to their credit, were also upset with Nelson's choice.

"Mom can't eat there, Dad! Why don't we go somewhere else?"

"Because *this* is where we're going."

We were all caught up in this standoff. Even though Nelson had started it, I had to figure out a way for all of us to finish it together. I ordered a salad and munched on crackers while my family ate their crabs. I was quiet and sullen as the menus were collected and the waitress asked if I was sure that was all I wanted. What I wanted was for my husband to understand me and give me his full and unconditional support, but I didn't think that was one of the house specials. I made a point of engaging the kids in animated conversation while ignoring Nelson. By the end of the meal, I was able to forgive him a little. He truly didn't understand what it meant to be serious about this and he couldn't believe that it might be so terribly important to me.

9/03/19

The Power of Religious Language

Mother's Day at the crabhouse was unpleasant, but I got through it. We all did. The kids learned about fortitude and determination and discipline. They now knew how strong my resolution was, and Nelson learned something about seriousness that didn't have to do with work or business. But I learned something about the resentment my behavior engendered. Nelson was trying to contain the range of my transformation by marking the boundaries for its incursions into our family life. It was one thing for me to undertake a personal religious odyssey, quite another for it to become a family expedition. Since *I* was clearly out of control, it was up to *him* to take over. My quest could take us only so far and no farther.

It's difficult to understand all the facets of religious transformation that make it so threatening to others. The very thing that made a serious commitment to Judaism so gratifying to me was what alarmed my family. They weren't too put out when I started to go to services. That choice didn't affect them much at all. It meant that the boys had to babysit for the girls on Saturday mornings; that the girls had to have a babysitter once both boys went off to college; and that I was unavailable for Saturday morning errands. Everyone was reasonably supportive as long as it was clear that I wouldn't make them go with me. When I started to attend the Shabbat afternoon study group, it meant that Nelson had to do more chauffeuring. My choice shifted new responsibilities to him. For nineteen years, he had been a free agent when it came to domestic responsibilities. Now I was changing the rules—not for us, but for *me*—and when I tried to explain why it was so important to me I only succeeded in frustrating myself and annoying him.

When I extended the Shabbat afternoon study group commitment to staying for *mincha* (afternoon) and *ma'ariv* (evening) services, Nelson got downright irritated. "Isn't that enough davening for one day? When is enough *enough*, Lee?" I couldn't answer him, because the question didn't make any sense to me. The reason I wanted to go wasn't about "enough davening." It was about having another

Jewish communal experience. I liked the informal intimacy of the chapel, the rapid-fire delivery of the opening *Amidah* prayers chanted by older men who had been doing it for years. I liked the *d'var Torah,* the brief teaching on the afternoon Torah portion—more a conversation between friends than a lesson. I enjoyed the feeling of being in a holy space as the sun set. Nothing special happened at home when the sun went down, except that Nelson and I started to get ready for whatever we had planned for the evening or we ordered a pizza, then hopped in the car to check out a movie from Blockbusters. In *shul,* I was made aware of time and its holy dimensions; at home, I was only aware of schedules and competing activities. When I tried to explain this to Nelson, it only annoyed him more. What was this "holy time" nonsense? Was I planning on becoming a nun? He knew a local order that took in lapsed virgins. I laughed because it was funny, but then realized that one of the major problems of religious transformation is vocabulary.

One of the great mistakes we have made in this country is ceding religious vocabulary to the religious right. As a result, our everyday language has become impoverished. We don't use words like "sacred," "holy," "covenantal," "divinity," "calling," "consecration," "redemption," "sanctification" and "God" anymore. Everyday discourse has become secularized with pop psychology taking the place of important religious ideas. We talk knowingly about "personal space," "self-esteem," "happiness," "self-actualization," "fulfillment," "victimization," "spirituality," "relationships" and "inner self," absolutely confident that everyone understands what we mean.

The problem is that pop psychology is *self*-centered while religion is *other*-centered. The vocabulary of pop psychology sets us *apart* from community while religious language draws us *into* community. But we are unable to appreciate or trust its power because the religious right has abused it so badly, using it to polarize and demonize—to break *down* community rather than build it *up.* When we hear religious words, we are immediately on guard, mistrusting the intent of the speaker, while our ignorance of the language prevents us from recognizing its legitimate use. Or we mistakenly think that the only people with a right to use religious language are clergy. That is because we have ceded religious *behavior* to our religious leaders. Anyone appropriating the clergy's exclusive vocabulary is therefore immediately suspect—an impostor until proven otherwise. If we expected religious behavior of ourselves, then we would *need* a religious vocabulary to talk about it with each another—just as we have created a pseudo-psychological vocabulary for talking publicly and unrelentingly about our emotional lives.

For Nelson, my new language was a dangerous form of jargon. It irritated, confused and frightened him because he thought that I might be using it as a tool for asserting moral and intellectual supe-riority or seizing the role of family leader. Like all specialized vocab-ularies, it had a predictable psychological effect: I knew the language. He didn't. I was in. He was out. It served as a regular re-minder of the choices I had made that he hadn't. I imagine there were times when he felt under siege, and he probably figured that if he just hunkered down and waited long enough, my fascination with religion and all its trappings would pass.

My kids knew better. Being kids, their antennae are tuned dif-ferently. They become expert early on in "reading" the adults who have power over their lives. They knew that serious change was afoot. They learned to listen carefully for key words that might sig-nal the onset of a "religious message," and they would roll their eyes and sigh, signaling their entrapment: "I'm stuck in this car with Mom and she's about to do her religious thing again." My religious "thing" wasn't directed *at* them. I wasn't trying to convert them or Nelson. It's just that I was changing so radically that I no longer saw the world the same way that I had. I was desperate to convey this shift to my husband and my children, but I didn't have the right tools. What I needed was a "bridge language," a way to connect what I was experiencing religiously with what they knew secularly, but I didn't know enough yet to pull that off. That didn't stop me from trying, but it meant that I usually failed to hold either their attention or their interest—which caused me much hurt and disappointment.

I vividly remember the second day of Rosh Hashanah in 1994. When I saw Rabbi Zaiman in the hallway after services, he innocently asked whose house I was going to for lunch afterwards. My throat burned as the loneliness of my decisions registered in a new way. The question shocked me. How could he *not* know that I had absolutely no one in my family to share a meal with? I was going home to an empty house on a day that was like any other day. Nelson was at work and the kids were all in school even though I had tried to convince everyone that we should be in *shul* together. I felt lonelier in that one moment than I had at any time since I had begun my Jewish journey, and I spent the afternoon feeling terribly sorry for myself. I finally resolved that self-pity would get me nowhere and decided that I had to try different tactics if there was any hope at all of involving my family. So I began to change the one religious ritual that was already institutionalized in our family life—Shabbat dinner— hoping to make it more meaningful for all of us.

Taking the Slow Train to Shabbat

When I married Nelson, directly after college, creating a Jewish home wasn't important to us. It did not occur to us to light the candles, say *kiddush* and break bread for ourselves, although we willingly participated if we were at either one of our family's houses for Friday night dinner. Even the arrival of children didn't change things until one Friday evening when we were supposed to drive to Washington D.C. for a formal banquet. Nelson arrived home looking exhausted. "You don't want to go, do you?" I asked. He admitted that he didn't, and I assured him that we wouldn't be missed at the enormous stand-up black tie event. He sighed with relief. Alex and Sam, who were then two and three-and-a-half, squealed with excitement.

"Let's do services!" Nelson suggested.

"Fine," I replied, a little surprised by the suggestion. After a quick scavenging session, I came up with a slice of white bread, a glass of grape juice, a pair of pewter candlesticks, two gently used dinner candles, three stray yarmulkes snagged from a rare *shul* visit and Nelson's *bar mitzvah* copy of *The Silverman Siddur*. We made Shabbat at the kitchen table. I have a real picture of it. For some reason, we both thought it was a Kodak moment worth recording.

For years, that picture remained static except for the addition of two more children, our daughters, Lindsay and Josepha, and a change of setting to the formal dining room in our current home. Our Shabbat dinner was usually thrown together from leftovers. And we rarely had a challah. Instead, we grabbed a slice of bread, a left-over hot dog roll, *anything* that would stand in as a substitute. Somewhere in those years, I added my father's prayer, "Thank you for the blessings of the past week and the privilege of being together again," an addition that connected my adult Shabbat to the Shabbat of my childhood. And Nelson regained mastery of the few prayers he remembered from his brotherhood days.

As our children grew older, there was a flexible rule around Shabbat: we expected them to be home for dinner . . . unless. Unless there was a sleepover, a special party, a school dance, a date. Nelson and I were less and less inclined over time to accept any invitations for ourselves for Friday nights—more because we were too tired at the end of week than that we had any special regard for Shabbat.

So our practice remained until I decided to change it. I began by making our Friday night dinner more of a special meal with better food and fresh flowers. A few months later, in halting, awkward Hebrew, I said the blessing for children for the first time which took *six* excruciatingly long minutes. Hesitantly, I reached out to touch the backs of our sons' and daughters' heads even as they pulled slightly away from me. The girls giggled, the boys smirked and Nelson shifted impatiently from one foot to another. I was acutely aware of how inept I appeared and equally aware how important that lesson was to my kids. When something is important to us, it doesn't matter how foolish or silly we may appear to others: We should do what we know is right. When I finished, I apologized for taking so long. One of the kids quipped, "No problem as long as we won't have to do *that* again!"

Everyone laughed and I mustered a weak smile. "But we will. Until I get it right."

"Aw, Mom! Dad, can't you *do* something?"

To my surprise, Nelson sided with me. "I think that was nice and I'm proud of your mother for trying." We were all uncomfortable. It was new and different and weird. But I continued to do it and they trusted me enough or loved me enough to tolerate it. Within a year, they were standing at my side as I recited the prayer in about twenty seconds, hands resting lovingly on the tops of their heads. Shabbat is no longer complete for me—or them—without it.

Our candlesticks expanded from one to three pairs as I purchased a set for each daughter while I was in Israel. Next, I ritualized the giving of *tzedakah* (money for charity) by handing the kids their weekly allowance before they came to the table. They took a portion of their choosing (I suggested ten percent, but didn't require it) and placed it in an antique brass humidor from my father-in-law which serves as our *tzedakah* box. Nelson and I each put in a few dollars as well. Once a year during Hanukkah, we decide together what cause to support with the money we've collected. One week, Nelson added to our celebration with a special sterling silver challah knife brought back from a business trip. While in Israel one year, I commissioned a challah cover that would match the colors of our dining room. And the challah we eat is the challah I've baked. The smell of baked bread fills the house every Friday evening and the kids come eagerly to the table for a slice of the still steaming loaf. What brain research now confirms Jewish mothers have known for centuries—association by aroma works! Eventually, I added the recitation of Micah 6:8, "It hath been told thee, oh man, what is good and what the Lord doth require of thee—only to do justly, to love mercy and to walk humbly with thy God." This is the only Torah my father ever quoted and the statement he believes captures the essence of Judaism.

Our most recent addition is for each person present to share one thing they are thankful for in the past week. It always surprises us that it is so hard to come up with that *one* thing—particularly for people who don't regularly think of events and other people as a source of blessing. I try from time to time to introduce a little Torah learning—and when I don't lead with my chin, it sometimes works.

Although I am still dissatisfied with the content of our Shabbat celebration, I know we are on a continuum. We've gotten on the slow train, but at least we know where we are going. We've gradually established a body of ritual intended to create an aura of specialness and anticipation that leads to holiness. Sometimes I cannot believe that, after four years, this is all we have accomplished. But then I remember that incremental change has a way of sticking while overnight change is often fleeting.

You've Got to Learn to Cry "Uncle"

Whenever my determination flags, I think about the great wrestling story in Torah. It follows one of the great dream stories. Jacob dreamed—and *then* Jacob wrestled. The sequence is essential. Torah seems to be saying that you have to be in the presence of angels to wrestle with them. You have to be *on* the ladder first. Like the minor changes in our Shabbat observance and the gradual changes in my own commitment to Judaism, the ladder has a built-in progression. In the many years that intervene between Jacob's prophetic dream and his epic all-night struggle, he's probably gone down that ladder as frequently as he's gone up. The physics of gravity apply equally to the logistics of holiness. What it doesn't seem possible to suggest is that he's ever gotten *off* the ladder. Once we are aware of the presence of God in our lives we can no longer deny the possibility of holiness in our days. We have to deal with what that means in terms of the decisions we make, the responsibilities we choose, the blessings our life represents.

As Jacob wrestled that night with an angel, he was transformed. Yet it is only when he *asks for and receives* his adversary's blessing that he can *cease* wrestling. He is transformed at that moment from "Jacob," someone who grasps and seizes at opportunities, to "Israel," one who creates and receives them. But it is the act of asking for and receiving a blessing that releases him from the obligation to wrestle indefinitely. In a way, he has to cry "Uncle!" How apt a metaphor that is for all of us who are wrestling with Judaism and its many requirements, challenges and satisfactions. Perhaps it is only when we are able to truly see the *mitzvot* as a blessing that we will be able to stop struggling against them and instead offer ourselves openly to their redemptive and renewing power. So what's stopping us? The same things that stopped me and that now stop my family: Our comfort with what we know; our learned behavior, acquired prejudices and desperate need to believe in the myth that we are the true authors of our destiny.

Consider for a moment how many of us could benefit from precisely the respite Shabbat offers. Yet how many of us consider it a blessing, not a monumental inconvenience? Think what it would mean to call a moratorium one day a week on phone calls, answering machines, meetings, errands, beepers, car pools, schedules. To let the day mark itself according to the natural progression of time and not the artificial structure we impose on it. How many of us know, apart from an occasional vacation, what it means to stop working? How many of us are capable of even making a distinction between work and *not* work? With faxes, cell phones, e-mail—instant and constant accessibility—how can we prevent the intrusion of work into every aspect of our lives? Are we afraid that we won't have an identity if we *don't* have work?

In *The Sabbath: Its Meaning for Modern Man,* Abraham Joshua Heschel writes, "The result of our *thinginess* is our blindness to all the reality that fails to identify itself as a thing, as a matter of fact. This is obvious in our understanding of time, which, being thingless and insubstantial, appears to us as if it had no reality. Indeed, we know what to do with space but do not know what to do about time, except to make it subservient to space. Most of us seem to labor for the sake of things of space. As a result, we suffer from a deeply rooted dread of time and stand aghast when compelled to look into its face."

That hits home for me. On the rare occasion when I walk out of the house without my watch, I experience high anxiety. I turn my empty forearm every ten to fifteen minutes to check the hour, then scan every room I enter for a clock. I feel incomplete, hobbled, distracted. This isn't holiness. It's insanity. And it's exactly what Heschel means. This is not about dedicating time to God; it's about slavishly devoting ourselves to schedules that have as their primary purpose the pursuit of "thinginess": a meeting or an errand completed, an appointment kept. We can live our lives with a fanatic commitment to that kind of time which has nothing to do with holiness—or we can acknowledge that, whatever may be demanded from us six days of the week, on the seventh day we are called to consciously invite God to infuse our lives with joy, purpose and holiness. Through Shabbat, we can better understand God's intentions, expectations and hopes for us.

After two years of struggling with Judaism, I knew I was on Jacob's ladder and I wanted my family to be on it with me. While I knew I didn't have the right to demand anything of my family, my dreams for them were changing. As my personal Jewish identity expanded, I encountered a gaping hole where family should be. I realized that I couldn't complete my dream without them, so I knew I needed to find more ways to share it with them. For all of us, staying on the ladder requires patience, fortitude and a high tolerance for setbacks. I had to be prepared for that and not horribly disappointed if setbacks did happen. When I proposed one day to Nelson that Shabbat might offer the very refuge he was looking for, the perfect vehicle for creating the family time he claimed we never had enough of, I triggered an angry response. He wasn't able to see it yet as a blessing—only as a sly way to manipulate him, an unfair request that put unreasonable demands on his schedule.

I encountered similar resistance when I tentatively explored the possibility of kashering our kitchen (making it kosher). What a ridiculous idea! Why deliberately conform to an arbitrary and inconvenient eating code? If we didn't live in the ghetto anymore, why did we still need the ghetto's cuisine? I knew that explanations about *kashrut* enabling us to distinguish ourselves from others by our dietary choices would fall on deaf ears, so I didn't try. But it was harder to maintain my own choices in the inhospitable environment Nelson's open disapproval created.

I kept chipping away at the things I could change without triggering too much active resistance. Josie's enthusiasm for *sukkah* construction didn't last out the year, so I had the synagogue-sponsored *sukkah* building group set up a *sukkah* at our home. I'll never forget Lindsay's reaction that afternoon when a friend brought her home. "God, Mom! You're not putting that thing on our lawn! You don't actually expect us to eat in it do you? I hope nobody sees it before you take it down. When *are* you taking it down?" A torrent of questions revealed her adolescent horror at putting evidence of our Jewish identity on our lawn for the whole world to see. In Lindsay's world, religion was decisively uncool. In the four years we have had a *sukkah,* we have shared perhaps seven meals in it as a family. But I keep setting it up and taking it down. One year we'll eat all our meals there. I'm not sure when, but I believe that it will happen.

The Hat Makes the Man

Nelson and the kids have watched with everything ranging from grudging admiration to outright disapproval as I've wrestled with the garb of religious belief. Like every other religion, Judaism has its own wardrobe accessories designed to tell other people this person is a believer and to help the believer strengthen their beliefs. I'll never forget my kids' wry smiles the morning I whisked into the den to say goodbye before Shabbat services. Alex looked up from the paper he was reading and offered a seemingly offhand, "Nice hat, Mom." This prompted a chorus of "Yeah, Mom, nice hat. You look good!" from the girls as well. Bless them! They knew not to ask why this morning was different from all other mornings. Why a hat on this day when on all other days I went hatless? If they had asked why I was doing this I would have been barely able to explain and I knew that any questions might have undone my still-shaky decision. After months of attending services, I woke up *this* particular morning with the desire to cover my head. For a full twenty minutes, I had stood in front of my mirror trying on the three hats I owned from a time when hats had been in vogue. The difference was that wearing a hat now wasn't a fashion statement, but a theological one. And I understand that once I made that statement publicly there would be no going back. To walk into my sanctuary wearing a hat would signal to the congregation, the community I belonged to, that I had arrived at yet another stage in my spiritual development. It would be a visible statement of my relationship to God and my reverence for the space in which we celebrated our communal relationship to God. To do it once without the intention of doing it forever would be folly. So the twenty minutes I spent in front of the mirror wasn't for primping; it was for soul-searching—the time I needed to dig down and determine that the impulse was a real one, and not a passing fancy. The kids were my first test, and with the peculiar sensitivity that kids have from doing the hard self-conscious work of developing their own identities, they knew exactly what not to do. But they also appreciated that it was a significant decision. When I returned home from services, I went straight to the kitchen with my hat still on since Josie had asked me to make her a grilled cheese sandwich as soon as I walked into the house. As I prepared it, she stood quietly by my side.

"What's up?" I asked.

"Mom, you're not going 'frummy' [traditional Orthodox] on us are you?"

I laughed and hugged her. "No, I'm not going 'frummy' on you, but it suddenly felt right to wear a hat. And I'm glad I did. *Shul* was different for me today. A little more special. I was more aware of the words I was saying. More conscious. . ."

"It's okay, Mom," she cut in, indicating that she wasn't interested in the full explanation—just the reassurance that certain boundaries were still intact. "Just as long as you don't go 'frummy' on us. And please . . . don't burn my sandwich."

Over the past few years, all the kids have become personal shoppers for me, keeping an eye out for hats and urging me to buy one that they think would look good on me. But while my family could handle hats, wearing a *tallit* (the prayer shawl Jews wear for daily prayer) was another issue altogether.

When I broached wearing a *tallit* in *shul* with Nelson, he was emphatically opposed.

"What do you want to do that for!" he groused. Sam had once teased him, "Dad, you're a nineties kind of guy." Nelson beamed, not aware that there was a punchline: "An *eighteen*-nineties kind of guy." And we all roared because it was so true. This remarkable man, renowned for thinking "outside of the box" as a medical professional, was quite conventional in his personal life. A romantic traditionalist, he reflexively resisted any action that challenged traditional role definitions. My wearing a *tallit* was definitely a role-challenging moment.

"I'm just thinking about it," I said. In truth *I* was struggling with it as well. I had deliberately chosen a hat over a *kippah* (skull cap) because I considered the *kippah* a male garment. A few women I admired were wearing a *tallit* comfortably and proudly every week in *shul*, but I couldn't get past the notion that wearing a *tallit* was like wearing a tie—something for guys, not women. I had thought about ways to customize a *tallit* to reflect my understanding of its purpose as well as to satisfy my female emotional and psychological needs. I had even commissioned a woman to make a sample of the *tallit* I had in mind. It would be woven from 613 horizontal threads that would represent the spectrum of the rainbow, with two to three strands for each new color. The rainbow warp would be interwoven with strands of copper, silver and gold. My *tallit* had a *midrash* behind it: the rainbow signified the incomplete covenant from the Noah story. God promised never to destroy the earth, and put a rainbow in the sky as a reminder. The problem, as I understood it, was that it was a *one-way* covenant because Noah, perhaps suffering from traumatic stress syndrome, had been silent in the face of God's monumental proclamation. Naamah, Noah's wife, was—as is often the case with wives in Torah—simply not there. She was probably still cleaning out the ark or giving the kids their breakfast. It didn't matter so much then, but it mattered tremendously now in the twentieth century when humankind possessed, for the first time, the power to utterly destroy the earth in one fell swoop. If we wanted to make the covenant a bilateral one, we would have to acknowledge that we had our own promise to make to God and the earth. I wanted to restore Naamah to my new reading of the story to be reminded of our unfinished business every time I prayed, so that I might find the inspiration to help complete it.

The copper, silver, and gold threads symbolized the precious metals the women were the first to donate when the *mishkan* (the portable holy tabernacle) was constructed in the desert after the Exodus. I wanted to remember that my foremothers rushed to fulfill their obligation while the men hung back. That they understood we all have something to contribute to communal holiness and we mustn't hesitate to give whatever we have when the opportunity presents itself. I had the sample. I had the *midrash*, but I wasn't ready to undertake the *mitzvah* of *tallit* and Nelson, even though he liked my *midrash*, did not like the idea of my assuming what he considered had always been a male prerogative. "Why don't you just wear a nice scarf instead? Scarves look good with hats."

Exasperated, I retorted, "You *know* that's not the point, sweetheart."

"I know," he said, "but I don't like the point."

And we dropped the discussion because I wasn't ready to press the point. The sample sits in a drawer in our dining room and every few months I pull it out to look at it. I wonder if it's garish or too didactic or too precious or contrived. I wonder when—or if—I'll ever be in the place that gives me not only the guts but the confidence and need not only to have the *tallit* made but to wear it. I do know that I'm not there yet and that the absence of family models and encouragement makes that distance a little farther and a little harder for me to travel.

A Thing of Beauty Is a Joy Forever

In truth, the absence of familial models has an effect that spills over into almost every area of the adult seeker's life. One of the hardest things for the newly observant Jew to figure out is how to make our homes into sacred spaces, because most of us have little to no experience with sanctification. Not in the New Age sense of creating personalized shrines replete with magical totems, but in the sense of making the home a place in which we are constantly aware of God's residence because we are regularly inviting God into it. A *mezuzah* on the doorpost and a pair of candlesticks on the table do not a sacred space make. A house is a home when it reflects its inhabitants' interests and commitments. But a home can become a sanctuary when it reflects its inhabitants' convictions. After three years there was still not enough evidence in our home to say that any of us were interested in, much less passionate about, Judaism.

My response to most Judaica, in direct inverse proportion to my growing desire to love it, was repulsion. I considered most of it either crude, ugly, tacky, gaudy, overwrought or sentimental. Nothing resonated with my fledgling expressions of what Judaism was coming to mean to me or the struggles I was having with making it meaningful until the day I met David Moss, an Israeli artist, and learned about his newest project. He talked about the "lost object" of Jewish ritual life, the lowly *shtender* of the bet *hatefillah* (house of prayer): the serviceable but plain wooden table that enables the davener to shuckle (rock back and forth as he prays) because he can lay his *siddur* (prayer book) down. David and his partner, Noah Greenberg, had the idea to create a *shtender* that would contain all the objects a Jew would need for a full year of daily, weekly and holiday ritual observance. The goal was to use every inch of space, to aim for the highest economy without sacrificing grace. The intent was to introduce intrigue, intimacy, mystery, playfulness into the trappings of ritual life. It was an intriguing concept but when David stopped talking and started to take the magnificent carved wood objects out of their nifty individual traveling cases, all skepticism disappeared and a childlike wonder took its place. Such beauty, such joy! To marry craft with purpose and tradition in such a determined yet imaginative way actually took my breath away. For the first time in my life I beheld a Jewish object, other than a book, that I simply *had* to have. I wanted to hold each piece, smell it, turn it over in my hands, feel the weight of it, grow into the purpose of it. I wanted to belong to the entire thing as much as I wanted it to belong to me—and I wanted to have one in my home.

When I told Nelson and the kids about it, my enthusiasm was almost infectious. They've never seen me so excited about a *thing*. Even though I paid for it, the decision to purchase it was the first major decision Nelson and I shared since I started my "odyssey" because our whole family would have to live with it—not just me. I believed intuitively that living with beautiful Jewish things could make a difference in our lives, and it turns out that I was right. My family loves these pieces. They are proud of their clever beauty and enjoy showing them to guests. The *shtender* itself is not here yet, but we have six of the objects it will eventually contain. We use the challah board and the *yahrtzeit* candle holder regularly. I didn't have the nerve to use the *chanukkiah,* the special eight-branched candelabrum used at Chanukah, because it is made of wood and has oil lamps; but Josie helped me to put my *lulav* in the *lulav* case and the *etrog* (citron, a citrus fruit that grows in the Middle East) in the *etrog* case during Sukkot this year. She is the only one who can load the wine cups into the special *kiddush* container carved with grape leaves. I can imagine her teaching her own child to do the same thing one day. It is the kind of object that gets effortlessly incorporated into family lore. Beautiful things dedicated to a sacred purpose have that special power. And every time I look at one of the objects I am reminded of God and the possibility that our home can become a place where others are aware of God as well.

Nelson and I still discuss theology and religion even though it's hard for both of us. He struggles to understand what I find in observance and study and I'm amazed that he just doesn't "get" it. We talk about it over coffee, during our daily morning walks, in the car. Because it's so much a part of my life, it comes up rather frequently—about as often as we discuss his frustrations as a doctor and his various business plans. He wants to understand what I find so compelling about religion when science is there for the taking.

I choose my words carefully, conscious that each conversation is crucial. I never know which one will finally contain the words that may reveal new meaning to him.

"Because," I say, "science believes in the power of man's intellect, while religion believes in the power of man's spirit. Religion believes in the mystery of the unknowable; science believes that we will eventually know all. Religion encourages us to make peace with uncertainty and science encourages us to believe that eventually we can eliminate uncertainty altogether. I think we're meant to live with mystery and uncertainty. That's a huge part of what makes life worth living. If everything's known or knowable, what happens to human desire and curiosity? What happens to dreams and vision? Why bother?"

"But what proof do you have that you're right?"

"None. Not in the way you mean. But sometimes things that are true can't be proven. Science is as much of a tyrant as religion, Nel.

The most important thing that Rabbi Zaiman has taught me is 'We're only as free as the master we serve allows us to be.'"

Once Nelson lashed out at the martyrology service (the Yom Kippur afternoon service that memorializes all the Jews who died for their beliefs). "What's the point. They all died! They can't help anyone once they're dead. Why didn't they fight instead? I would have fought."

I have to think about that one for a minute. I'm not a big fan of martyrdom myself. "I'm not sure," I say, "but I think it works like this. There are certain truths so compelling that they become your stake *in* life, but they move to another level of significance altogether when you realize you'd stake your life *on* them. What meaning does life have if there aren't things we would live and die for?"

Other times we discuss theology. "Do you really believe that the world was created because God said so?"

"Yes and no. I believe in a divine scheme lying at the heart of the universe's existence. Look, science affirms that all life really did come from one initial source. Human beings are just a combination of . . . ?"

"Hydrogen, oxygen, carbon, nitrogen, calcium, sodium, potassium, essential amino acids, RNA and DNA."

"So we could be a clod of dirt, but we're not. How else can we explain earth's incredible diversity and beauty other than to ascribe it to some divine creative force? Could any of *us* have thought this up and planned for the thousands of ecosystems that hold this planet together? The genius of it is far beyond human capacity."

Or mythology versus the historical accuracy of Torah.

"Do you really believe in the revelation at Mount Sinai?"

"No, but it's a great story! It places community right at the heart of our faith."

It hasn't been easy or painless to pursue all this amid an indifferent and sometimes openly hostile family environment. What makes it worthwhile is hoping that one day my family will take these same things as seriously as I do. Not so that I will stop feeling lonely and isolated, but so that they will not be strangers to their own magnificent tradition, and their lives will be as enriched by Judaism as mine has been.

I do much less talking than modeling these days. Doing the things you believe in is a more powerful lesson than talking about them. So I do *teshuvah* (atonement) with my family before Yom Kippur: I apologize for the wrongs I have done them during the past year, vow to change and ask for their forgiveness. The first time I did it was incredibly difficult. The third time it was easier. I don't do it expecting them to return the *mitzvah,* but this year Nelson did. Perhaps next year, he will initiate it. The rhythm of the Jewish calendar now regulates my life and my family is aware of it every time they consult the kitchen calendar and see the Jewish holidays and *shul* events inscribed across the days and nights of our year. I have had a modest influence on our *sedarim,* modeling the second night *seder* in our home on the ancient Roman symposia. We lounge about on cushions and use grab bags filled with everyday objects, a fixed set of questions or the device of the old campfire game, "the pot's boiling over," to enable us to fulfill the commandment of telling the story. And at last year's first night family *seder* when the new *Haggadah* we were using didn't work because it required too much knowledge about the structure of the service, everyone turned to me for help. I stood up and led the kids in an exercise that wove theology and narrative together. It was the first time that we, as a family, departed from the text and had someone knowledgeable enough to guide the departure.

I use Torah to teach the kids moral lessons and I'm very clear that that's where my moral authority comes from. When Josie got in trouble for being a distraction in school, we talked about the prohibitions in the Jewish tradition against interfering with learning. When Lindsay related a complex situation regarding another child's experimentation with drugs and illegal driving and his friends' unwillingness to tell an adult about the situation, we discussed the Jewish commandment to save a life. Endangering a friendship is secondary to endangering a life—an incredibly powerful message for a teenager wrestling with peer pressure, autonomy and adult authority.

Most significantly, my notions of relationships and community have changed. I now view relationships within an ethical rather than a psychological framework. If something's gone awry in a relationship, my first inclination is to look for a rupture in values, a breaking of covenant. Likewise, I understand communities differently. I know how they should work when they honor their members—and I can tell pretty quickly which communities (family, school, congregational, political, non-profit) have that essential integrity. I have learned that the stories we tell are the stories that tell us who we are. So I try to be a better storyteller both at home and in the community. I recognize the remarkable power of religious vocabulary and religious ideas and try to harness and use that power properly and wisely. I have a much greater reverence for the minority opinion than I might simply as a student of democracy. Seeing the dissenting views of the great rabbis preserved for centuries in the pages of Talmud has given added weight to the importance of safeguarding the minority voice—whether it be from one of my children or a fellow board member. I am more conscious of all the stumbling blocks we put in the way of others and of our obligation to remove them. And in perhaps the most significant accomplishment for our family, Nelson has agreed to attend the Florence Melton Adult Mini-School at our synagogue. Developed at Hebrew University in Jerusalem, the two-year curriculum covers a wide range of Jewish subject matter. Setting aside two hours every week is an important commitment for each of us. But taking the course together represents a new kind of commitment to our marriage and to our family and to Judaism. Since he loves me, Nelson simply did not want to obstruct my choices any longer.

Transformation of individuals and families is long, hard work. After all, it took forty years in the desert for a new generation of leaders to emerge who could conquer and settle Canaan. A crisis may jumpstart us into action, but crises can't sustain the momentum necessary for true transformation. Only people can do that—through vision, energy and determination. But we risk losing our vision and squandering our energy and determination when we encounter hostility from our families and indifference from our communities.

According to *Baba Metzia* 59b, the commandment to treat the stranger well appears thirty-six times in Torah—more than any other *mitzvah*. From this, our sages deduced that it is one of the most challenging commandments to honor. Their insights into our tendency to oppress the "other" or to ignore their plight are remarkable. But perhaps the saddest commentary of all is the modern commentary— the one we are now writing with our own lives. Perhaps there is no greater indication of the toll that assimilation has taken on Jewish life in America than the fact that our families *do* see us as strangers and our religious communities do *not* know how to reach out to us and support us. For probably much too long, we are strangers in both places and far more alone than our tradition or God ever intended us to be.

9

Spirituality, Schmerituality: Getting There through Deeds

Effort is its own reward. We are here to do. And through doing to learn; and through learning to know; and through knowing to experience wonder; and through wonder to attain wisdom; and through wisdom to find simplicity; and through simplicity to give attention; and through attention to see what needs to be done. . . .

—Pirke Avot V:27

I admit it. I don't like the word "spirituality." I mistrust it. I'm not even sure what it means, but I know I resent it when people assume their understanding of it is the same as mine. "Oh, Lee's on a spiritual quest," they declare, as if they were describing an adolescent's attempt to "find herself." Consigning me to that category conveniently explains my engagement with Judaism, making it intensely personal and, therefore, entirely capricious. They exile me to the land of self-absorption, when, in fact, what I think I am doing is the exact opposite of exile and self-absorption.

I admire precision in language. When we settle for ambiguity, we forego mastery and deny the crucial impulse to make meaning of our lives. The purpose of all language is to create—and to communicate—meaning within a particular context. So we ought to be able to assume consistent definitions for critical words, words that communicate something significant about need or place. "Spirituality" strikes me as one of those words. But I haven't the faintest notion what most people mean when they use it. Is their imprecision intentional or unavoidable? Or is it that no one word can possibly capture all the nuance and complexity of this complicated idea?

Are they talking about some sort of out-of-body experience, a way to escape the constraints of time and place? Are they thinking about a moment when they lose their sense of self, a temporary loss necessary for them to experience a higher level of "being"? Are they referring to a moment of awe, usually triggered by some natural phenomenon that stops us dead in our tracks? Are they referring to the possibility of encountering divinity: catching a glimpse of God or finding that God's purpose for them has suddenly been revealed?

My sense is that people mean all of the above and more: what we mean depends on the occasion. We are not only talking about an experience, but a possibility, about "spirituality" as a means of getting from one place to another. We're also talking about spirituality as a goal, the place we will know when we get there. We use the two applications interchangeably without regard for distinctions. It's become a catch-all term to encompass all that's elusive in our lives—our deepest emotions, yearnings and impulses—and its indiscriminate use obscures the very meaning we're struggling to establish.

The one thing I'm certain of is that spirituality is not something I can *seek*. It's something that comes *to* me when I am purposefully pursuing the knowledge and acts that grant life meaning. Going in search of it is as fruitless as setting out on a journey to "find" myself. If that's all I'm after, that is all I'll find: a self-contained universe; a biosphere of one. Individuals "in search of themselves" bore and annoy me. They have so little to share, so little to contribute from all those hours spent on themselves. They are as narcissistic as fitness fanatics and seldom as pretty to look at. When I encounter one of them, a refrain from my parents goes round and round in my head: "Don't bother looking in your belly button. All you'll find is your belly button." While their folk wisdom wasn't intended to encourage soul-searching introspection, they did teach me to be ruthlessly honest with myself and to value deed over intent—to be spirited, but not spiritual. My whole upbringing—and my natural disposition—inclined me to learn by doing, to seek meaning by exercising whatever gifts

I've been graced with, to trust in them enough (because they are *God's* gifts and only on loan to me) to go where they lead me.

In his book *Flow,* Mihaly Csikszentmihalyi, a professor of psychology and education at the University of Chicago, describes a unique state of being. "Flow," as he defines it, is the pinnacle of human experience. Athletes, writers, dancers, artists, women in labor all experience it. It occurs when we are so deeply focused and concentrated on a task that we lose all self-consciousness. We transcend self by creating, doing, being. Unanticipated interruptions, heightened self-consciousness, pain, and time constraints all disrupt "flow," depriving us of the uniquely gratifying (perhaps holy) energy and sense of well-being that "flow" creates. But when we experience the *full* effect of "flow," it is the nearest we ever come to discovering our essential humanity, our reason for being.

This is the closest enunciation of spirituality I have encountered—and the most sensible one. For me, spirituality is what happens when mind, body and soul are all in the same place at the same time; when these three elements of self are so fully present and integrated that internal boundaries dissolve, and we suddenly "see" in a different way. It is that rare moment when we turn to face life utterly whole and complete—totally capable of being in *that* instant. It is a moment of sacred coherence. This is not, as some might suggest, a mindless exercise. Rather, it comes from being mind*ful,* from vigorously exercising our intellectual and creative powers to the point that we can stop thinking about them. It is that state where purpose displaces desire, like riding a bike and getting beyond the aching in your legs to the point where you can pedal painlessly, persistently. It is that moment when you can glory in the ride and no longer *think* about it.

The Jewish Soul I Didn't Know I Had

What does this definition of "spirituality" have to do with Judaism? It gives me a framework for understanding not only the profound attraction, but the deep satisfaction I have found in Judaism. It explains almost every form of joy and growth I have experienced in the past four years: All those times I have lost myself in learning, doing, praying—and felt energized and almost exalted. This is an odd thing to admit since I have steadfastly maintained that I am *not* on a "spiritual journey." I didn't want to be pigeonholed and stuffed into some cramped space of another's imagining. That possibility inferred that much of what was happening was happening *to* me rather than *because* of me and my active engagement with Judaism. If that's what "spirituality" meant to others—a kind of holy passivity—then I didn't want it pinned on me or on Judaism. That wasn't what I sought when I started out, and it's not what I'm after now that I've moved a tiny distance from my initial point of embarkation.

I certainly did not understand this at the outset. Ironically, it took a conversation with a Christian to force me to rethink my take on "spirituality." My good friend, Peter, invited me for one of his famous "teas" on a weekday afternoon in the fall of 1993. Peter is the only American male I know who can issue an invitation for tea without sounding affected. Approaching sixty, he has a lanky, thin body and an appealing boyish face. I've known Peter for seventeen years since I first served on the board of Center Stage, the theater where he has been managing director for over three decades. Peter and I may be kindred spirits in our love of theater, and our faith in the essential goodness of people. Yet for the many years we've known each other, I didn't know how deeply religious he was. It had never come up. What Peter wanted during our two-hour tea was to explore how I felt about Judaism and what my experience meant to my family. We sat at a table in his kitchen, slowly sipping our freshly brewed iced tea.

"Do your children have any sense of what you are going through?"

"Only in the way that kids sense everything: by how it affects their lives. Mom's not available for errands on Saturday mornings any more. We can't do soccer league."

I laughed, then dug a little deeper. "No, that's not entirely true. Sam is paying attention. He says he is learning from me that adults can keep growing. And the girls are now enrolled in religious school. Alex is quiet. He's watching and taking it all in. I expect to hear his reaction about four years from now."

He laughed and then asked me about "spirituality." I rolled my eyes. Like a car accidentally turning onto a dead-end street, Peter backed up and looked for another way around. He wanted to know *when* I experience spirituality.

"Peter, I'm not even sure I know what that *is!* I think I may have seen it in some Christians, but I don't know if it's really possible for Jews."

"Well then, do you feel the presence of God when you study Torah?"

I smiled. "You flatter me. Not yet. I haven't studied enough. In fact, I've hardly studied at all. And I may never experience it. Not even then."

"Do you feel God when you're out in nature?"

"Yes, there I feel God. There, I can make myself empty, but that emptiness doesn't feel to me as if it's particularly Jewish—or rather *specifically* Jewish. I think it's natural. The universal response of any human being who's paying attention."

"Do you know the presence of God anywhere else?"

That one stumped me for a moment. This was the first time I had reflected on "spirituality" other than to vigorously deny it when people suggested I was pursuing it. Somehow I was willing to do with Peter what I had refused to do with anyone else. Peter was not so easy to dismiss for he wasn't trying to pin me down: He was trying to understand me. That realization let me take his question seriously and honestly consider it for the first time. I idly stirred my drink, then finally looked at Peter. "I sense God when I'm writing and an idea goes *through* me. It doesn't come *from* me. That's a moment of inspiration. Maybe," I whispered, "it's the feeling of God breathing on my neck."

I became excited as I realized I was suddenly saying something that was true, not speculative: "When I'm no longer thinking but *doing,* I become the vehicle through which an idea moves. I don't feel like I can take any credit for what comes out then, only for being there. And even if I could leave, I wouldn't be able to. Something much bigger than me holds me there. I have to *stay* with it. In some way, it is a holy moment."

Peter understood what I meant because he had heard similar

...om all kinds of artists. But he still hadn't gotten what he was after. "How about grace, Lee? What do you know of grace?"

I sighed. "How about grace! All I know about grace is 'There but for the grace of God go I.' Which is different from what you mean, I think."

"And passion?" he asked. "Passion and . . . Judaism?"

"We are passionate about learning and teaching. When we are learning and teaching, God is present."

"So then, can't you be passionate about God?"

I was surprised at my instant response. "Oh no, I don't think so, Peter! That feels dangerously close to idolatry! When you have a passion for something, it's so easy to make the mistake of thinking you can control the thing you are passionate about."

"Do you believe in a personal God?"

That one got me. I'd been struggling with that very question as the High Holy Days approached and I'd taken the standard post-Holocaust position: "I can't make sense of a personal God in tandem with the Holocaust." Peter nodded respectfully. I was entitled to my alienation.

"How about religious joy? Have you ever experienced joy while in the synagogue?" At that point, I could only think of one time when this had happened: At a *tikkun* program, an evening of community study on the eve of Shavuot, that I had attended the previous May, serenity had enveloped the entire sanctuary, uniting everyone simultaneously to the same purpose. I shut my eyes as the feeling washed over me and was surprised by the visual image that came to me: cherubim fluttering near the ceiling, holding the four corners of a transparent canopy above us—so magical that we couldn't feel its weight, only its presence. For the first time, I had understood the refrain "Holy, holy, holy is the Lord of hosts," and was transported as the community together created a sacred moment that I hadn't witnessed before or since.

"Joy is hard to achieve in our sanctuary, Peter. It's not designed to encourage it and our services don't elicit it. Judaism is a cerebral religion that occupies the intellect first and the spirit second—if at all. We seek faith through the brain. Blind obedience is okay, but observance that comes from knowledge is better."

And so it went: Peter enabling me to confront what no one else could. Talking with him gave me a different perspective. The differences between us let us ask questions of each other that our co-religionists would never have presumed to ask. He made me think about things I would rather take for granted or just ignore. I think what he was really after was my Jewish soul, and my answers to all his questions began to convince me that I might have one. 9/7/18

I was beginning to reassess my relationship with God. I couldn't keep believing that I had *personally* experienced God through my own creativity, while also maintaining my post-Holocaust theological view that God had contracted after the birth of mankind and retreated into the distance. Which was it: a God who had abandoned the field of history to man—or the God who breathed on our necks when we forgot who we were in the act of creating? A God who parted the heavens from the earth and then disappeared—or the God who brought my people out from Egypt and worked through history? I couldn't figure out how to have it both ways. Perhaps even more importantly, I was no longer sure that I *wanted* it both ways. Did I want to resign myself to the absolute capriciousness of fate—or figure out how to believe in a God whose mysterious and awesome power I had *some* chance of understanding through Torah? It wasn't a reconciliation I was after, but a revelation.

Having a Relationship with God

On the next Yom Kippur, the one that occurred in October of 1993, I spent the entire day in synagogue, knowing what I had to do. I needed to take a journey without any guarantee that I would reach my destination. I needed to give up, give in, let go. I needed to cry. And I did that on and off for the first five hours of the service. I needed to find a way to connect with God so I could experience a crucial aspect of *teshuvah,* that aspect of repentance that is achieved by turning toward or returning to God, and thereby experience the possibility of God's forgiveness. I needed that so I could begin the year with a clean slate. But I realized that possibility was beyond my reach if I didn't believe in a personal God. Why turn to and ask forgiveness of a God you don't believe is listening?

With Peter's help, I had finally begun to admit to myself how instinctive my exploration of Judaism actually was, not so much a planned expedition as a spontaneous adventure. I felt a childlike delight in discovering a new love: the synagogue. I had taken pleasure in the realization that adults can still grow like children. I was not innocent, but I had been ignorant when I began my journey. I hadn't been responsible for my original ignorance, but I was responsible for "fixing" it once I had acknowledged the problem. So I went to synagogue week after week, learning the rituals, acquiring the rhythm, enjoying the community, devouring the Torah lessons, reacting to the sermons. I wasn't acritical in this process. Ignorance wasn't an excuse for intellectual passivity. If anything, ignorance in adulthood put a greater onus on me to think as I learned.

I was moving forward. I had almost entirely reformulated my sense of what it means to be Jewish. My new definition had substance. I felt the heft of its logic. It seemed so patently obvious to me that I couldn't believe I had been so blind to it before: We *are* the people of the covenant. And we are chosen because we *accepted* the covenantal relationship with God. The nature of the relationship, its rules and guidelines are all laid out in Torah. To be a Jew means to accept responsibility for that relationship. To do that *responsibly,* a Jew has to know Torah because Torah binds us to each other and to God. We can't be Jews outside of Torah and pass on our traditions, because, without Torah, we *have* no tradition to pass on. We may have customs, activities, rituals, cultural memories but, without Torah, we lose our history—*and* the source of our history. Nothing survives without a history and the means to invoke and transmit it. Our story as a people is in Torah, and we invoke and transmit it through study, worship and the performance of *mitzvot.*

More and more, I realized how little credit I could take for turning to synagogue when I did. That was mostly an instinctive act; but conscious or unconscious, deliberate or instinctive, I'd accomplished a lot. Even so, I knew I was missing something essential and I was growing increasingly impatient with myself because I sensed it must be an obvious important thing that I was just too dense or stubborn to see. My rabbi challenged me just two days before Yom Kippur. When he said that "holding the Holocaust as a reason for not believing in a personal God is the biggest cop-out I know," I knew he was right. Did I want a relationship with God—or just the excuse not to have one? I was growing tired of all the excuses I had fabricated. They were so convoluted and contradictory—and what effort it took to sustain them! All those hurdles between me and the truth. I had to maintain constant intellectual vigilance to continually leap over them. 09/10 118

The cop-out challenge did it. In *shul* that day, I realized that I was *scared* to have a personal relationship with God. If I did, then I had the right to expect things from God, and perhaps more importantly, God had the right to expect things from *me*. I would have to be accountable to a higher authority than myself and the world of family and community that I was so comfortable with. I knew that I usually resisted and resented authority. I'd challenged it, mistrusted it, or protected myself from it all my life because it was often arbitrary, cruel, unthinking or unfeeling. But who was I to judge or mistrust God's authority? God's authority was not arbitrary, it was knowable through Torah. If I chose to study Torah, I could learn to understand God's authority. I was God's instrument on earth, and chosen for a purpose: to do God's work, to be a member of "a holy people," to complete the task of repairing the world. I didn't have to personify God in order to have a personal relationship with the divine. God could take whatever form God needed in order to be a personal God because *God* needed the relationship as much as I did. That realization was simultaneously startling, enlivening, frightening.

I cried on and off throughout Yom Kippur services that day. My *Al Cheyt*, the prayer we recite as a community that enumerates our personal and communal failings in the context of community during the previous year, was for the sin of keeping God out of my heart. I traveled from despair to a gentle joy and truly felt forgiven at day's end. I had never understood the possibility or the power of *teshuvah* before. Of course, if you don't believe in a personal God, there is no possibility and no power. Rabbi Zaiman and others counseled me in the following months to ease up and slow down. But I knew I wasn't entirely in charge of either my appetite or my energy. I was stepping into the field of sacred relationships and encountering forces more powerful than any I'd experienced.

At the *Neilah* (closing) services of Yom Kippur, we imagine the gates of judgment swinging shut as the final judgment on our individual and collective fates in the coming year is determined. In the months after, it was as if I had walked through that one set of gates just before they clanged shut and I continued to walk through a series of successive gates—each one opening up new and powerful possibilities as my own theology expanded to embrace the possibility of an active, engaged and personal God.

Relationships Are All We've Got

Now nearly four years later, I am less impatient when people use the word "spirituality" around me. I'm more willing to hear what they mean, not so trigger-happy and ready to either denounce or trounce them. My study of Genesis and my growing understanding of *halachah*, Jewish law, and the role it plays in our lives have gradually expanded my notion of Jewish spirituality. Today, I believe there is such a thing as "spirituality," but it's different than what my friend, Peter, and other people were after. It's about a oneness that we spend all of our lives trying to achieve—or, perhaps, trying to recover. It's not the Christian notion of reversing the fall from grace or trying to redeem ourselves afterwards. It's an impulse deeply embedded in Jewish texts and reaffirmed through our liturgy: A sense that there once was—and can be again—a state of universal harmony, one that each of us can know and experience. It will directly inform us about why we were put on earth and how to fulfill that purpose. We will know it because the din of ugliness and corruption ("The earth became corrupt before God; the earth was filled with lawlessness," Genesis 6:11) will no longer drown out the possibility of hearing God. We will know it because we will be attracted to good, not continually distracted by evil. We will know it because everyone and everything on earth will be performing from the same score—in their own style, to be sure, but with the shared intent of making music together—less an orchestrated symphonic performance than a spontaneous jazz riff. And we can achieve it *by working to get there*.

Genesis contains two Creation stories. One story tells us that we are made in God's image, *b'zelim elohim*. This principle still grounds Jewish relations with all of humanity and with our fellow Jews. The second story (we are meant to connect the two) gives us the remarkable notion of God breathing life into the first human, who is, according to rabbinic legend, at that point, male-female. The first story seems to be saying: Remember that we are all made in God's image; that we all came from the same gene pool; and that a long, long time ago, we all spoke the same language and lived in harmony with all of creation. The ancient idea of our coming from one place in time and space may explain the enduring human fantasy to return to that place where chaos is banished and peace prevails. The myth gives us a guide for present behavior—and a dream to work on for our future.

The guide? If we are all made in God's image then all our interactions contain the possibility of a divine encounter, a possibility that must frame our actions and elevate our ethics from the realm of "it would be nice" to the world of "shalts" and "shalt nots." Ethical behavior, as an expression of our original and continuing divinity, can invest our lives with Godliness—continuing divine meaning and purpose.

The dream? The notion of paradise is a universal fantasy—a recurring archetype expressed by every culture in one way or another. Judaism reinterprets this archetype in a specifically Jewish way by saying that the paradise of Genesis manifests a divinely ordained hierarchy which derives from God's oneness. It also says that God's judgment of goodness ("and God saw that it was good") relies on a planned, innate balance (day-and-night, heaven-and-earth, crawling-and-flying creatures) and relates the power of language directly to creation. With words, we may create worlds. With words we may dream of improvements we would like to make. Through deeds, we make those improvements.

Is it possible that the second Creation story taps into an almost ineffable yearning to *be* inspired, to have life breathed into us by a divine source, to know from the inside out that our life is divine? And couldn't the route to that inspiration in Judaism be *through* Torah? If Torah is the word of God and if we keep Torah alive in our lives and minds and hearts, isn't it then possible to continually reaffirm God's original role in our creation by drawing divine inspiration from Torah? As a Jew, the way to do that is by bringing Torah into our lives through study, prayer, and action. These activities correlate directly to mind, soul and body. The quest to understand and unify these elements of our humanity leads us to a life of wholeness and sacred coherence. Together, study, prayer and action help to organize, focus and steady us in the midst of a chaotic world that constantly threatens us with distractions, temptations and distortions.

The point, of course, is to fulfill the ancient commandment to be holy like God, to individually and collectively fulfill the original promise of being made in God's image. That is what I seek. I am not looking for a spiritual recovery program to reclaim my lost inner self. I don't care to give voice to my primal scream because I don't think it would be a very pretty sound. I don't want to get in touch with "the child within" because I'm an adult who got there by going through childhood. I'm interested in forward movement, not self-indulgent back-pedaling. I'm trying to bring prayer, study and action, meaningfully, sincerely and fully into my public life *and* my private life: to live them, believe them and breathe them. Then perhaps one day, the breath of God I once felt on the back of my neck will be the breath of God in my own lungs, inspiring me with every inhalation to do good deeds, to stand for the right things, to love humanity and to work to make the world a better place than when I found it.

I can't do that by sitting around and examining my belly button, as my parents so gruffly maintained. I can't do it by communing with trees and birds and hoping for a glorious, "natural" moment of divine revelation, although that doesn't mean that God is absent from nature. God *is* in the physics of a raindrop and the design of a daffodil. Anyone who cares to look can see that. But God is also in the vortex of a tornado and the thorn of a rose. Neither recognition requires much of me unless I'm a meteorologist or a botanist or have the bad luck to be standing in the path of a funnel cloud or to have carelessly clutched a sweetheart bouquet. Certainly, I can relate to God through nature—and I do. But I can't have a *full* relationship with God there unless I choose to set up housekeeping in a cave and live off the land. I like my creature comforts. I love electricity and furniture and indoor plumbing and telephones and computers. I love my family. I love my community. I love this world we live in, awful as it sometimes is. And I love my God. In every instance, my love requires me to have a relationship with the other: home, family, community, world, God. And when you have a relationship with someone or something you have to take responsibility for your share of it.

Seeing What Needs to Be Done

For me, spirituality is the natural byproduct of taking responsibility for those relationships. It is not a state of transcendence we achieve through passivity, because taking responsibility for something requires us to *do*. Antoine de St.-Exupéry captures this idea exquisitely in his timeless children's tale, *The Little Prince*. In the story, Antoine, a downed airplane pilot, encounters a mysterious little boy in the desert who recounts his interplanetary adventures and the instruction he's received from a variety of teachers. An extraordinarily gentle but wise soul, the child finally learns from a fox the lesson that lets him make sense out of his trials and end his self-imposed exile: "It is only with the heart that one can see rightly, what is essential is invisible to the eye. . . . It is the time you have wasted for your rose that makes your rose so important. Men have forgotten this truth, but you must not forget it. You become responsible forever for what you have tamed. You are responsible for your rose. . . ."

I don't know of any other way to maintain or sustain a meaningful relationship of any kind except to take responsibility for it. I know that *thinking* about my responsibilities, engaging in quiet, honest reflection, may help me better hold up my end of the bargain. I know that what I feel often influences what *I* do. But since I have yet to master the art of telekenesis I have yet to see my feelings change a single thing or a single soul outside of myself. Feelings seldom change the world, but actions *always* do. I don't want to live in a world in which I have to depend on my neighbor's *feelings* to predict her behavior. I do want to be part of a community in which everyone feels *obligated* to behave in a certain way. With obligation as the prevailing rule of conduct, I can count on others to do the right thing and they can count on me to do the same, regardless of how we feel, because safeguarding the sanctity of the community is *more important* than our individual emotional needs at any point in time. How can there be a community of common intention and integrity if everyone does what they think is right *only* when it "feels" right for them or *only* when it makes them feel good about themselves? How can we know what will make one person feel good about themselves and another awful? How can we measure human conduct by that standard? How can we depend upon each another if we are all hostages to mood and motivation? The simple answer is that we can't. Torah acknowledges that truth. We wouldn't need commandments if we all *felt* like doing them. It's precisely because we don't always feel like it that we *need* them. That's why we're *commanded* to do them. We are obliged, and that means "have to"—*not* "may—if I feel like it that particular day." Obligation is just another word for responsibility and responsibilities don't go away simply because we grow tired of them or find them too difficult to assume. Our ability to shoulder responsibility willingly, kindly and wisely is the litmus test of our continuing growth and development as human beings. Obedience as a manifestation of responsibility is a profound expression of our respect for other people and our reverence for God; a recognition that all our actions have consequences and that all our relationships have a holy dimension. The law of cause and effect is immutable whether in physics or human behavior.

I can discover the wholeness of spirit, the fullness of purpose, the exaltation of coherence—the spirituality that *I* seek—when I pursue every relationship I have with all my heart (which is "mind" in the rabbinic tradition), with all my soul and with all my might (which is "body"). Judaism commands me to seek those relationships *in* community and to link heart, soul and might to study, prayer and action through Torah. The moments when I get the linkages right will be moments of "spirituality." If I can string the moments together one after another and learn to sustain and connect them, I will be living a life of *Jewish* spirituality. Torah will tell me how to do it. But the pursuit requires, as *Pirke Avot* reminds us, that

I do, *"and through doing to learn; and through learning to know; and through knowing to experience wonder; and through wonder to attain wisdom; and through wisdom to find simplicity; and through simplicity to give attention; and through attention to see what needs to be done. . . ."*

[handwritten notes:]

call Katie at the VA

not going on Wed.
will be on the
Art Show
instead
+ get well.

call Annika
Black
+ tell her
I didn't know
my cell phone
was full
full
I shall help
her cut out
things for her
bulletin board
another time
if she would
like.

I'm overbooked
+ overwhelmed

Acknowledgments

I did not know when I began that writing a book about my religious experience would *be* a religious experience. I am thankful to Jewish Lights Publishing and Stuart Matlins for having faith in the possibilities of this story and for giving me the opportunity to testify.

I am especially grateful to:

My husband, Nelson, for his unfailing honesty and continuing encouragement. Aware that his portrait was, at times, less than flattering, his generosity of spirit and unswerving commitment to telling it "like it was" enabled me to write a truthful book. I love him all the more for it.

My children Sam, Alex, Lindsay, and Josepha for their forbearance, love, laughter, reactions, and understanding. They are great kids. Without them, the story couldn't have been written.

My father, Bud Meyerhoff, for a lifetime of examples and love, my sisters, Terry Rubenstein and her husband, Jim, Zoh Hieronimus and her husband, Bob, and my brother, Joe Meyerhoff and his wife, Jennifer, for their interest, suggestions and support.

My editor, Arthur Magida, who introduced me kindly but unrelentingly to the rigors of editing. His insight, skill and discipline helped me to transform a raw and rambling manuscript into a book. Never adversarial, but always direct, he created a collaborative partnership that let me learn and grow. No author could expect more.

My teachers, Dr. Louis L. Kaplan, who planted the conviction in me as a child that there is wonder and excitement in Jewish learning, and Rabbi Joel H. Zaiman, who brought that wonder and excitement to life in my adulthood. Rarely does one encounter a master teacher. To have been touched by two in one lifetime is a true blessing. My deep gratitude also to Rabbi Zaiman for readings of successive drafts, and his probing criticism and sustained interest in this project from beginning to end.

Leslie Thomas, my right-hand person and incredibly competent and efficient assistant. When she taught me how to use a computer six years ago, my life changed forever. I am indebted to her for her kindness, hard work, and careful attention to detail, and for helping me in so many ways—large and small.

Ron Wolfson for giving me the idea for this book in the first place and for calling me regularly until I took him up on it.

The members of my Women's Torah Study group for five years of shared joy in study.

Darrell Friedman for helping me to grow by seeing something in me that I did not see myself, and giving me a wonderful opportunity and a push.

Linda Blumenthal, Carol Kleinman, Peter Culman, Dan Pekarsky and Dr. David Teutsch for readings of sections of the manuscript and for their helpful feedback.

Judy Meltzer and Ann Zaiman for their thoughtful readings of the very first draft.

Nessa Rappoport for her reading of an early draft and her detailed, insightful suggestions.

Angela Munitz for her enthusiasm and careful reading of a late draft of the book.

Eli Evans for his gentle encouragement.

The talented professionals and laymen of the Council for Initiatives in Jewish Education for enlarging my vision of Jewish education and for helping me to translate my passion for learning into philanthropic action.

Joanne Kraus and Barry Lever for being models. They were the first serious adult Jewish learners I encountered at Chizuk Amuno. Their mastery was impressive and their dedication was inspiring. I will always remember their strong encouragement and example.

My congregation, Chizuk Amuno, for providing such a magnificent and vibrant Jewish community for me to join.

Other significant teachers (I am better for their influence): Marjorie Terrell, Elsie Trumbo, Elaine Salabes, Jenifer Carsiotes, Ruth Read, Edith Russell, Dorothy Graham, Herbert Morss, Les Harris, Ethel Schlessinger, Allen Turner, Joanna Spiro, Ellen Deese, Elizabeth Weingartner, Ruth Spahn, Midge Thursby, Kenneth Greif, Brooks Lakin, Jack Russell, George Dalsheimer, Dr. Thomas McCullough, Dr. Eric Meyers, Dr. Carol Meyers, Dr. Herbert Metz, Dr. Richard Palmer, Dr. Parvin S. Sharpless, Dr. David Jackson, Louise Mehta, Jean O'Barr, Carol Gilligan, Rabbi Richard Camras, Rabbi Stuart Seltzer, Dr. Moshe Shualy, Marietta Jaffe, Dr. Chaim Botwinick, Rabbi Louis Hoffman, Dr. Peter Pitzele, Reverend Chris Leighton, Roseanne Catalano, David Moss, Noam Zion, Rabbi Gustav Buchdahl, Rabbi Nina Beth Cardin, Michael Wegier, and Avram Infeld.

Appendix

Where Do I Start? A Guide to Beginning a Jewish Home Library

Many people have asked me the same question that *I* asked when I began my Jewish journey: "Where do I start?" Apart from advising people to join a learning community—a study group, a congregation or a free-standing institution for Jewish learning—the next most important suggestion I can make is to start building a Jewish home library.

For many people, the first Jewish learning community they will join is the virtual one available on the Internet. It is, in many cases, a fine place to start, but please be cautious about the chat rooms you enter and the teachers you learn with. *Everyone* has an agenda. Try to determine whether your net partner's agenda is the same as yours. Are they interested in brainwashing and spoon-feeding or in genuine inquiry and learning? Are they taking advantage of your ignorance and vulnerability or respecting your autonomy and skill as a learning adult? Are they encouraging or condescending? Beware of overly simplistic, reductive explanations. Try to distinguish between dogmatic, doctrinal offerings and authentic ones that require you to think and question. Much preferable, if possible, is to find a qualified teacher with whom you can learn in your own community. The Internet, in the final analysis, cannot substitute for flesh-and-blood encounters just as a CD-ROM library is no substitute for a real library with books you can feel, smell, and underline.

Below are some books that were especially helpful to me when I started to read Jewishly. The last three listings came to my attention after I finished this book, but I wish I had studied them much earlier.

The JPS (Jewish Publication Society) Torah Commentary:
    Sarna, Nahum N. *Genesis*. New York: The Jewish Publication Society, 1989.
    Sarna, Nahum N. *Exodus*. New York: The Jewish Publication Society, 1991.
    Levine, Baruch A. *Leviticus*. New York: The Jewish Publication Society, 1989.
    Milgrom, Jacob. *Numbers*. New York: The Jewish Publication Society, 1989.
    Tigay, Jeffrey H. *Deuteronomy*. New York: The Jewish Publication Society, 1996.

The foundation of a Jewish library is the Five Books of Moses. There's nothing like going to the source and getting to know it from the inside out. These five volumes are the most comprehensive and wide-ranging Torah translation and commentary for the modern adult learner. Enlightened, erudite, straightforward but complex, the commentaries work on multiple levels at once. At first, they may confuse you with their wealth of information, but their value becomes evident as you use them more and more. The scholarship, analysis and historical information meet the highest standards. These gems do not come cheap. Each volume runs between $45 and $60.

Plaut, W. Gunther. *The Torah: A Modern Commentary*. New York: Union of American Hebrew Congregations, 1981.

Another comprehensive edition of Torah. You're really on your way toward building a Jewish library when you have more than one Torah translation and commentary. It's impossible to study Torah well unless you have access to multiple voices. Having more than one voice on your bookshelf is also a physical reminder of the multiplicity of views that Torah is meant to inspire. The organization of this volume with "gleanings"—relevant, brief writings from Jewish sages, contemporary Jewish thinkers and Christian and Moslem writers—at the end of each

major chapter helps the reader to appreciate what's most important
and how universal Torah's impact is.

**Fox, Everett. *The Five Books of Moses*. New York: Schocken
Books, 1995.**

If your tastes run to the literary, try this magnificent translation of the
Pentateuch. There's much less commentary than in the other two
versions, but Fox's insights are especially incisive and astute. And the
English, in his hands, acquires an arresting quality that most other
translations miss. Read it aloud and you will get some sense of how
Torah sounds and what it means when it's read in Hebrew.

**Heschel, Abraham Joshua. *The Sabbath: Its Meaning for
Modern Man*. New York: Farrar, Straus, Giroux, 1995.**

When I first read this book, I didn't get it. By the third reading, it
began to sink in. A brilliant treatise on the meaning of Shabbat, it is
all the more stunning when you discover that Heschel only learned
English when he came to America as an adult. His command of the
language is exhilarating. As you grow, it will grow with you. A book
to read again and again.

**Holtz, Barry W., editor. *Back to the Sources*. New York: Summit
Books, 1984.**

A wonderfully-edited collection of essays that explain the major
sources in Jewish tradition. It demystifies a confusing landscape,
teaching the reader the differences between Midrash and Talmud;
and explaining the development and significance of such texts as the
medieval commentaries, kabbalistic writings and the prayer book.
This is another book you will return to as your knowledge and understanding grow.

**Kushner, Lawrence. *The Book of Letters: A Mystical Hebrew
Alphabet*. Woodstock, Vt.: Jewish Lights Publishing, 1990.**

Rabbi Kushner, a prolific contemporary writer, has produced many
manuscripts of note, but this is one of my favorites. You know your
ABCs. Now you have to learn your aleph beit. Only this is learning

with a difference—not a rote memorization, but an unlocking of Jewish tradition that reveals the mystery and power of the Hebrew alphabet. This slim volume is beautifully conceived in a layout that mimics a page of Talmud; you get the text—that is, the letter in question—with wide-ranging commentary surrounding it. Kushner makes the letters dance and he'll make your mind dance too. Kushner believes that spirituality isn't a dead art, but an ongoing quest that each of us can undertake when we study seriously and look through Jewish eyes at the wonder of the world around us. Appreciating the meaning and mystical dimensions of the Hebrew alphabet is one of the first steps you can take to expand your vision.

Simon, Ethelyn, editor. *Prayerbook Hebrew the Easy Way.* Oakland, Calif.: EKS Publishing Company, 1985.

If you have no idea what the prayers mean but can read Hebrew (even at the beginner's level), this is a great book. Carefully structured and user-friendly, it helps you learn the basics of prayer book grammar and sentence structure. If you really *do* the exercises, you will be rewarded with a basic prayer book literacy. Within a year (or far less if you're more disciplined and diligent than I), you will begin to understand much more of what you are praying.

Steinberg, Milton. *As a Driven Leaf.* West Orange, N.J.: Behrman House, 1996.

This classic work of fiction does more to illuminate the world of ancient Rabbinic tradition than anything else I've read. Taking place during the Roman occupation of Palestine immediately following the destruction of the second temple (70 C.E.) this compelling novel affirms that Jewish sages wrestled as bravely with trying to find the meaning of life and the purpose of faith as any other great sages throughout world history. The difference is that they wrestled by engaging in an active dialogue with a sacred text, making it come alive and assuring that, through the structures and systems they established, it would remain alive even to this day.

Telushkin, Joseph. *Jewish Literacy*. New York: William Morrow and Co., 1991.

The book jacket reads: "The most important things to know about the Jewish religion, its people and its history." I imagine the claim is hyperbolic, but I certainly learned many important things from this book. Well-organized and well-written, it's a quick and easy source for answers to countless questions about Jewish customs, practices, characters, values and historical events. If you can't afford an *Encyclopedia Judaica*, this is a good starter reference to have in your library.

Greenberg, Irving. *The Jewish Way*. New York: Simon and Schuster, 1988.

Using the Jewish holidays as his springboard, Greenberg extracts from their texts and observance the essential Jewish values and tenets that give meaning and shape to our lives. By turns lyrical, scholarly, provocative and down-to-earth, this wonderful book will make you think—and think again. Whatever they taught you in Sunday school about the Jewish holidays probably missed the mark. In the hands of Greenberg, our holidays come alive—filled with wonder, mystery, pathos and powerful ritual. Learning more about them will lead you to *doing* more about them. As a teacher, Greenberg is as good as they get.

Plaskow, Judith. *Standing Again at Sinai*. San Francisco: HarperSanFrancisco, 1990.

I don't feel that, as a woman, I've been written out of the tradition as much as Plaskow does. But then I haven't studied the texts the way she has. Carefully researched, persuasively written, Plaskow raises all the right questions. Where *were* the women at Sinai? Why *are* all the images of God in our sacred writings so unrelentingly male? What does the treatment of women as sexual objects in Judaism do to their humanity? How has the exclusion of women from Jewish public ritual life deprived our community of their special gifts and strengths? As a Jewish woman, you can't *not* read this book. As a Jewish man, if you want to have a better understanding of Jewish women, it's a must read for you too.

Wolfson, Ron. *The Art of Jewish Living: The Shabbat Seder*. Woodstock, Vt.: Jewish Lights Publishing, 1996.

This is a warm and engaging how-to primer. If you want to try to make the Shabbat meal a more meaningful experience, this is a great place to start. Lacing inspiring pictures, real-life stories, solid teaching and commentary throughout, Wolfson gently guides you down the path to more confident observance. Breaking down the order, or *seder* in Hebrew, of the meal, there's step-by-step practical advice for every stage. Incorporating comments from families like yours and mine, prayer transliterations and clear explanations, Wolfson uses humor, honesty and education to encourage you to risk trying something new. Try it, then move on to Wolfson's three other books: *Hanukkah; The Passover Seder;* and *A Time to Mourn, A Time to Comfort: A Guide to Jewish Bereavement and Comfort* (Jewish Lights).

Bialik, Hayyim Nachman and Ravnitzky, Yehoshua Hana. *The Book of Legends: Sefer Ha-aggadah*. New York: Schocken Books, 1992.

Baffling at first, *Sefer Ha-aggadah* is another book that becomes indispensable when knowing what our sages thought and felt about any number of vital issues matters to you. An impressive volume, it reflects the remarkable collaboration of the famous Hebrew poet, Bialik, and the editor, Ravnitsky. Grouped thematically around Jewish values—like hospitality and leadership—the collected stories from Midrash and Talmud, which are called *aggadot* in Hebrew, reveal the lively rabbinic dialogue that takes place across centuries as our sages interpret Torah. It may seem weird and fanciful at first—and then you begin to get it. Having a study partner helps.

Gillman, Neil. *Sacred Fragments: Recovering Theology for the Modern Jew*. New York: The Jewish Publication Society, 1990.

This book was specifically written for an adult lay audience to address the fundamental theological questions every modern adult Jew confronts. Remarkably readable even when Gillman deals with the most complex and confusing challenges, he asserts that we can all find a working personal theology for ourselves. A gifted analyst and synthesizer, he makes each of the great modern philosophical movements accessible. The most powerful lesson I took from this book is that myths are true even when they haven't actually occurred. When you understand that truth, Torah leaps to life and remains forever relevant.

Frankel, Ellen and Teutsch, Betsy Platkin. *The Encyclopedia of Jewish Symbols*. **Northvale, N.J.: Jason Aronson, 1992.**

This exceptional resource provides thoughtful but succinct explanations of over 250 objects, events, people or places that have aquired symbolic significance in Jewish life. Careful cross-referencing enables the reader to see how the listings relate to one another. Clear language dispels many misunderstandings and the authors pay special attention to the spiritual dimension of each listing.

Neusner, Jacob. *The Enchantments of Judaism*. **New York: Basic Books, 1987.**

Neusner is not an easy read and he doesn't try to be. He works through the structures and meanings of the basic rites of Judaism when experienced individually and communally. The beauty of Judaism is that it enchants us with the moral and spiritual choreography of its rites and rituals. Unfortunately, Neusner maintains, we have lost our ability to experience that enchantment communally. He argues that we must retrieve it to experience the full magic and mystery of our tradition. At once inspiring and disturbing, a careful reading will make you ask new questions of yourself and your community.

Moss, David. *The Moss Haggadah*. **New York: Bet Alpha Editions, 1990.**

A remarkable blend of *midrash* and artistic genius, this book demonstrates how beautiful Judaica works on multiple levels. Through the use of reproductions, calligraphy and original art, Moss shows us the richness of the story of our redemption from slavery in Egypt that freed us to serve God, and how we have learned to see and understand it through the centuries. His research and insights are impressive, his creative interpretations even more so. This is a true work of art. Every Jewish home needs a *Haggadah*. Make this the one that becomes a family heirloom.

Klein, Isaac. *A Guide to Jewish Religious Practice*. New York: The Jewish Theological Seminary of America, 1979.

You want the laws and the rationale regarding religious observance and you want them straight? This book is particularly good if you are attracted to Conservative Judaism, but it is useful no matter what your denominational persuasion.

Harlow, Jules. *Siddur Sim Shalom*. New York: The Rabbinical Assembly, The United Synagogue of America, 1985.

You can't have a Jewish library without a Jewish prayer book. This happens to be the prayer book that my congregation uses. I have others from the Reform (*Gates of Prayer,* ed. Chaim Stern, New York: Central Conference of American Rabbis, 1975), Reconstructionist (*Kol Haneshamah: Shabbat v'Chagim,* ed. David A. Teutsch, Wyncote, Pa.: Reconstructionist Press, 1994) and Orthodox (*Siddur Ahavas Shalom,* ed. Nosson Scherman, Brooklyn, N.Y.: Mesorah Publications, 1984) movements, but this is the one I usually turn to because it's the one I've come to know. Without a prayer book, you haven't got a prayer of understanding what prayer is supposed to mean in our lives or how to make it a part of yours. Get one and study it. You'll be surprised at some of the other things that are in it besides prayer, such as *Pirke Avot* and contemporary reflections on the Holocaust and the act of prayer.

Dresner, Samuel H., Siegel, Seymour and Pollock, David M. *The Jewish Dietary Laws*. New York: The Rabbinical Assembly of America and United Synagogue Commission on Jewish Education, 1982.

The rules and the reasons for observing *kashrut*. It's an easy read without being overly simplistic or dogmatic. The myths you most likely learned about the kosher dietary laws are wrong. This book might give you the courage and the information you need to consider committing yourself more to this *mitzvah*.

Orenstein, Debra, editor. *Lifecycles, V. 1: Jewish Women on Life Passages and Personal Milestones; V. 2: Jewish Women on Biblical Themes in Contemporary Life*. Woodstock, Vt.: Jewish Lights Publishing, 1994 and 1997.

These are the first two volumes in a projected three-volume series: practical guides that connect feminist sensitivities and scholarship to real-life events. "Sharing" (both our joy and our sorrow) is sometimes overrated in this collection of wide-ranging contributions from Jewish female scholars, religious leaders and laywomen, but the net effect is one of ever-increasing possibility: we *can* craft new rituals and we *can* make them meaningful. And we can do it in an authentically Jewish way.

Graetz, Heinrich. *History of the Jews*, 6 volumes. Philadelphia: The Jewish Publication Society of America, 1949.

A great history written fifty years ago about events that took place centuries ago is still a great history today. Graetz is the consummate historian—painstaking in his facts and his consideration of political, economic and social issues. Whenever I've turned to this text, I've been rewarded with clear explanations and very little editorializing.

Frankel, Ellen, editor. *The Jewish Spirit: A Celebration in Stories and Art*. New York: Stewart, Tabori & Chang, 1997.

We Jews love telling stories of all kinds. This wonderful, whimsical collection features stories from around the world—from ancient Jewish folktales to classic modern short stories. True to its name, it celebrates the irrepressible Jewish spirit. The pairing of literary entries (thematically organized) with an equally diverse sampling of quality work by Jewish artists makes this book a true treasure. It's a coffee-table book and a night-table book all in one.

Wolpe, David J. *Why Be Jewish?* **New York: Henry Holt and Company, 1995.**

This slim volume packs a wallop. It matches in truly contemporary spirit the interpretive skill of the great synthesizers of our tradition. Wolpe examines Judaism through the dual lens of our tradition and our American experience—using familiar images and idioms that we can immediately understand. A friend recently gave me his extra copy while showing me through his Jewish library. "Here," he said, "this is a really good book. You should have it." It *is* a really good book. You should have it too.

Gordis, Daniel. *Does the World Need the Jews?* **New York: Scribner, 1997.**

Another young rabbi takes a crack at *the* question. Like a heat-seeking missile, Gordis goes after the ambivalence and ambiguity that lie at the roots of our American Jewish identity. Making a forceful and compelling case, and citing Jewish text and recent historical events, Gordis argues that it's not good enough to simply *claim* our Jewish identity. We have to live it, breathe it, know it and drop all pretense of thinking we can preserve a tradition without committing ourselves distinctly and seriously to it. Do this, Gordis challenges, and your life will become more meaningful as a Jew *and* as an American.

Glossary

Akedah: the biblical commandment to Abraham to offer Isaac as a sacrifice.

Akiva: Rabbi Akiva ben Joseph (C.E. 50?–132) whose scholarship, particularly a reinterpretation of *halachah,* profoundly influenced Judaism.

aliyah: literally, "going up"; the term used for the person being called to "go up" from the congregation to say the Torah blessings while the Torah is being read.

Amidah: "the standing prayer," one of the two central prayers in most Jewish services.

bar mitzvah: "son of the commandment"; the age at which Jewish tradition considers a boy religiously responsible for his acts; and by extension, the ceremony celebrating his achieving that status, and generally held around his thirteenth birthday.

bat mitzvah: "daughter of the commandment"; the age at which Jewish tradition considers a girl religiously responsible for her acts; and by extension, the ceremony celebrating her achieving that status, and generally held around her twelfth or thirteenth birthday.

Bereshit: "In the beginning"; the Hebrew name for the Book of Genesis.

bimah: the raised platform in the sanctuary from which the Torah is read, and where the leader of the service stands while leading services.

bris: the Yiddish short form for *brit milah,* literally, "covenant of circumcision"; the ceremony of circumcision.

Chanukah: the Festival of Light, usually falling in December, and commemorating the victory of the Maccabees in 167 B.C.E.

chanukkiah: the special eight-branched candelabrum used at Chanukah.

chavurah: an independent Jewish fellowship group, existing as an alternative to the fully structured synagogue and emphasizing radical egalitarian democracy of all its members; or, a semi-independent study or prayer group within a synagogue or school.

chazzan: a cantor, who sings parts of the prayer service and leads the congregation in song.

Chumash: book containing the first five books of the Hebrew Bible (Genesis, Exodus, Leviticus, Numbers and Deuteronomy). Sometimes also contains the section from Prophets which is associated with each Torah section.

daven: the traditional style of Jewish worship, and a word often used instead of the English "pray."

d'var Torah: a short sermon or homily on the Torah portion of the week.

etrog: a citron (lemon-like fruit) used on Sukkot, the harvest festival.

gabbai: a lay person who oversees the honors and process of reading from the Torah and of saying blessings for the Torah reading.

Haftarah: the reading from Prophets at Sabbath and festival services.

Haggadah (pl. Haggadot): "the telling"; the text containing the ordered readings of the Passover *seder.* The Haggadah was originally conceived by the Rabbis to help parents fulfill the commandment to tell the story of Passover.

halachah: Jewish law.

High Holy Days: Rosh Hashanah and Yom Kippur; the ten-day period in between is known as the Ten Days of Repentance.

kashrut: the dietary laws (laws of keeping kosher).

kavannah: intentionality, especially in prayer.

kiddush: the prayer accompanied by wine or grape juice and recited before dinner on the eve of the Sabbath or a festival, to inaugurate the day and proclaim its sanctity.

kosher: food that may be eaten according to the dietary laws; also used to describe someone who keeps those laws, i.e. "someone who keeps kosher."

lulav: ceremonial "bouquet" of branches (palm, willow, and myrtle), waved during the rituals for Sukkot, the harvest festival.

machzor: High Holy Days prayer book.

matzah: unleavened bread required to be eaten during Passover.

menorah: a seven- or eight-branched candelabrum; if the latter (properly termed a *chanukkiah*), it is used expressly to hold Chanukah candles.

mezuzah: ritual object which contains the first two verses of the *Shema;* it is affixed to the doorway of Jewish homes as a reminder of righteous behavior.

midrash (pl. midrashim): a story or interpretation that tries to answer questions which the terse biblical text raises; legend in the Rabbinic style.

mitzvah (pl. mitzvot): one of the 613 commandments that Torah obliges Jews to fulfill. (A number of these, however, are no longer relevant since the destruction of the Temple.)

Pesach: the festival of Passover, commemorating the Exodus from Egypt.

Pidyon Haben: the traditional ritual of the redemption of the first-born son.

Pirke Avot: Literally, "Chapters of the Fathers," but often referred to as "Ethics of the Fathers." A collection of pithy sayings from the Talmudic era, about 200 B.C.E.–500 C.E.

Purim: the festival commemorating the victory of the Jews over their would-be murderer, Haman, as described in the biblical Book of Esther.

Rosh Hashanah: the Jewish New Year.

seder (pl. sedarim): the Passover evening meal and ritual through which the story of the Jewish people's liberation from slavery in Egypt, the Exodus, is told.

Shabbat: the Hebrew word for "Sabbath," from a word meaning "to rest."

Shavuot: the Festival of Weeks, commemorating the giving of Torah on Mount Sinai.

Shema: perhaps the most famous Jewish prayer, the biblical exclamation affirming the monotheistic principal: "Hear O Israel, the Eternal is our God, the Eternal is One."

shiva: literally, "seven," referring to the seven days of mourning following the death of an immediate relative.

shofar: the ram's horn sounded during worship on the New Year.

shul: the Yiddish word for "synagogue."

siddur: the prayer book.

Simchat Torah: the festival following Sukkot, marking the conclusion of one year's cycle of Torah readings and the beginning of another.

sukkah: the temporary shelter for eating and sleeping in made to use during the festival of Sukkot.

Sukkot: the harvest festival marked by erecting booths and thanking God for the food of the earth.

Talmud: the most famous collection of Jewish teaching, assembled over the years from the third to seventh centuries.

Tanakh: the Hebrew name for the Bible, an acronym comprised of Torah (the first five books), *Neviim* (Prophets), and *Ketuvim* (other writings).

tefillah: literally, prayer, but used more specifically for the *Amidah* prayer as "the prayer."

teshuvah: "returning"; repentance; Jews speak of "doing *teshuvah.*"

Torah: scroll containing the first five books of the Hebrew Bible.

Sometimes used more broadly to refer to a larger body of Jewish sacred writings.

tzedakah: charity; more broadly, the use of money to advance justice in the world.

Yad Vashem: the Holocaust memorial in Israel.

yahrtzeit: the anniversary of the death of an immediate relative.

yeshiva: an institute of learning where students study Judaism and Jewish texts.

Yom Kippur: the Day of Atonement, on which one engages in reflection and prayer and formally repents for sins committed during the previous Hebrew year.

About JEWISH LIGHTS Publishing

People of all faiths and backgrounds yearn for books that attract, engage, educate and spiritually inspire.

Our principal goal is to stimulate thought and help all people learn about who the Jewish People are, where they come from, and what the future can be made to hold. While people of our diverse Jewish heritage are the primary audience, our books speak to people in the Christian world as well and will broaden their understanding of Judaism and the roots of their own faith.

We bring to you authors who are at the forefront of spiritual thought and experience. While each has something different to say, they all say it in a voice that you can hear.

Our books are designed to welcome you and then to engage, stimulate and inspire. We judge our success not only by whether or not our books are beautiful and commercially successful, but by whether or not they make a difference in your life.

We at Jewish Lights take great care to produce beautiful books that present meaningful spiritual content in a form that reflects the art of making high quality books. Therefore, we want to acknowledge those who contributed to the production of this book.

PRODUCTION
Bronwen Battaglia

EDITORIAL & PROOFREADING
Jennifer Goneau & Martha McKinney

COVER DESIGN
Bronwen Battaglia

COVER/TEXT PRINTING AND BINDING
Lake Book, Melrose Park, Illinois

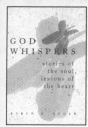

Spirituality

HOW TO BE A PERFECT STRANGER, In 2 Volumes
A Guide to Etiquette in Other People's Religious Ceremonies

Edited by *Stuart M. Matlins & Arthur J. Magida*

"A book that belongs in every living room, library and office!"

Explains the rituals and celebrations of America's major religions/denominations, helping an interested guest to feel comfortable, participate to the fullest extent possible, and avoid violating anyone's religious principles.

•AWARD WINNER•

Answers practical questions from the perspective of *any* other faith.

VOL. 1: America's Largest Faiths

VOL. 1 COVERS: Assemblies of God • Baptist • Buddhist • Christian Science • Churches of Christ • Disciples of Christ • Episcopalian • Greek Orthodox • Hindu • Islam • Jehovah's Witnesses • Jewish • Lutheran • Methodist • Mormon • Presbyterian • Quaker • Roman Catholic • Seventh-day Adventist • United Church of Christ

6" x 9", 432 pp. Hardcover, ISBN 1-879045-39-7 **$24.95**

VOL. 2: Other Faiths in America

VOL. 2 COVERS: African American Methodist Churches • Baha'i • Christian and Missionary Alliance • Christian Congregation • Church of the Brethren • Church of the Nazarene • Evangelical Free Church of America • International Church of the Foursquare Gospel • International Pentecostal Holiness Church • Mennonite/Amish • Native American • Orthodox Churches • Pentecostal Church of God • Reformed Church of America • Sikh • Unitarian Universalist • Wesleyan

6" x 9", 416 pp. HC, ISBN 1-879045-63-X **$24.95**

GOD & THE BIG BANG
Discovering Harmony Between Science & Spirituality
by *Daniel C. Matt*

Mysticism and science: What do they have in common? How can one enlighten the other? By drawing on modern cosmology and ancient Kabbalah, Matt shows how science and religion can together enrich our spiritual awareness and help us recover a sense of wonder and find our place in the universe.

"This poetic new book...helps us to understand the human meaning of creation."
—*Joel Primack, leading cosmologist, Professor of Physics, University of California, Santa Cruz*

•AWARD WINNER•

6" x 9", 216 pp. Quality Paperback, ISBN 1-879045-89-3 **$16.95**; HC, ISBN-48-6 **$21.95**

MINDING THE TEMPLE OF THE SOUL
Balancing Body, Mind, & Spirit through Traditional Jewish Prayer, Movement, & Meditation
by *Tamar Frankiel* and *Judy Greenfeld*

This new spiritual approach to physical health introduces readers to a spiritual tradition that affirms the body and enables them to reconceive their bodies in a more positive light. Relying on Kabbalistic teachings and other Jewish traditions, it shows us how to be more responsible for our own psychological and physical health. Focuses on the discipline of prayer, simple Tai Chi–like exercises and body positions, and guides the reader throughout, step-by-step, with diagrams, sketches and meditations.

7"x 10", 184 pp. Quality Paperback Original, illus., ISBN 1-879045-64-8 **$16.95**

Audiotape of the Blessings, Movements & Meditations (60-min. cassette) **$9.95**
Videotape of the Movements & Meditations (46-min. VHS) **$20.00**

Spirituality

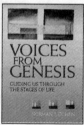

MEDITATION FROM THE HEART OF JUDAISM
Today's Teachers Share Their Practices, Techniques, and Faith
Edited by *Avram Davis*

A "how-to" guide for both beginning and experienced meditators, it will help you start meditating or help you enhance your practice.

Twenty-two masters of meditation explain why and how they meditate. *A detailed compendium of the experts' "Best Practices"* offers practical advice and starting points.

6" x 9", 256 pp. Quality Paperback, ISBN 1-58023-049-0 **$16.95**

HC, ISBN 1-879045-77-X **$21.95**

SELF, STRUGGLE & CHANGE
Family Conflict Stories in Genesis and Their Healing Insights for Our Lives
by *Norman J. Cohen*

How do I find greater wholeness in my life and in my family's life?

The people described by the biblical writers of Genesis were in situations and relationships very much like our own. We identify with them. Their stories still speak to us because they are about the same problems we deal with every day. Here a modern master of biblical interpretation brings us greater understanding of the ancient text and of ourselves in this intriguing re-telling of conflict between husband and wife, father and son, brothers, and sisters.

6" x 9", 224 pp. Quality Paperback, ISBN 1-879045-66-4 **$16.95**; HC, ISBN-19-2 **$21.95**

VOICES FROM GENESIS
Guiding Us Through the Stages of Life
by *Norman J. Cohen*

A brilliant blending of modern midrash and the life stages of Erik Erikson's developmental psychology. Shows how the pathways of our lives are quite similar to those of the leading figures of Genesis who speak directly to us, telling of their spiritual and emotional journeys.

6" x 9", 192 pp. HC, ISBN 1-879045-75-3 **$21.95**

ISRAEL—A SPIRITUAL TRAVEL GUIDE
A Companion for the Modern Jewish Pilgrim
by *Rabbi Lawrence A. Hoffman*

Be spiritually prepared for your journey to Israel.

A Jewish spiritual travel guide to Israel, helping today's pilgrim tap into the deep spiritual meaning of the ancient—and modern—sites of the Holy Land. Combines in quick reference format ancient blessings, medieval prayers, biblical and historical references, and modern poetry. The only guidebook that helps readers to prepare spiritually for the occasion. More than a guide book: It is a spiritual map.

4¾" x 10", 256 pp. Quality Paperback Original, ISBN 1-879045-56-7 **$18.95**   •AWARD WINNER•

Spirituality—The Kushner Series

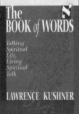

Spirituality

GOD WAS IN THIS PLACE & I, i DID NOT KNOW
Finding Self, Spirituality & Ultimate Meaning
by *Lawrence Kushner*

Who am I? Who is God? Kushner creates inspiring interpretations of Jacob's dream in Genesis, opening a window into Jewish spirituality for people of all faiths and backgrounds.

6" x 9", 192 pp. Quality Paperback, ISBN 1-879045-33-8 **$16.95**

THE RIVER OF LIGHT
Spirituality, Judaism, Consciousness
by *Lawrence Kushner*

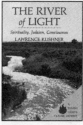

A "manual" for all spiritual travelers who would attempt a spiritual journey in our times. Taking us step by step, Kushner allows us to discover the meaning of our own quest: "to allow the river of light—the deepest currents of consciousness—to rise to the surface and animate our lives."

6" x 9", 180 pp. Quality Paperback, ISBN 1-879045-03-6 **$14.95**

GODWRESTLING—ROUND 2
Ancient Wisdom, Future Paths
by *Arthur Waskow*

This 20th-anniversary sequel to a seminal book of the Jewish renewal movement deals with spirituality in relation to personal growth, marriage, ecology, feminism, politics, and more.

6" x 9", 352 pp. Quality Paperback, ISBN 1-879045-72-9 **$18.95**
HC, ISBN -45-1 **$23.95**

•AWARD WINNER•

ECOLOGY & THE JEWISH SPIRIT
Where Nature & the Sacred Meet
Edited and with Introductions by *Ellen Bernstein*
What is nature's place in our spiritual lives?

A focus on nature is part of the fabric of Jewish thought. Here, experts bring us a richer understanding of the long-neglected themes of nature that are woven through the biblical creation story, ancient texts, traditional law, the holiday cycles, prayer, *mitzvot* (good deeds), and community.

6" x 9", 288 pp. HC, ISBN 1-879045-88-5 **$23.95**

BEING GOD'S PARTNER
How to Find the Hidden Link Between
Spirituality and Your Work
by *Jeffrey K. Salkin*; Introduction by *Norman Lear*

Will challenge people of every denomination to reconcile the cares of work and soul. A groundbreaking book about spirituality and the work world, from a Jewish perspective. Offers practical suggestions for balancing your professional life and spiritual self.

6" x 9", 192 pp. Quality Paperback, ISBN 1-879045-65-6 **$16.95**
HC, ISBN -37-0 **$19.95**

Spirituality

MY PEOPLE'S PRAYER BOOK
Traditional Prayers, Modern Commentaries
Vol. 1—The *Sh'ma* and Its Blessings
Vol. 2—The *Amidah*
Vol. 3—*P'sukei D'zimrah* (Morning Psalms)
Edited by *Rabbi Lawrence A. Hoffman*

Provides a diverse and exciting commentary to the traditional liturgy, written by 10 of today's most respected scholars and teachers from all perspectives of the Jewish world.

With 7 volumes published semiannually until completion of the series, this stunning work enables all of us to be involved in a personal dialogue with God, history and tradition through the heritage of the prayer book. "This book engages the mind and heart. . . . It challenges one's assumptions at whatever level of understanding one brings to the text." —*Jewish Herald-Voice*

Vol. 1: 7" x 10", 168 pp. HC, ISBN 1-879045-79-6 **$21.95**
Vol. 2: 7" x 10", 240 pp. HC, ISBN 1-879045-80-X **$21.95**
Vol. 3: 7" x 10", 192 pp. (est.) HC, ISBN 1-879045-81-8 **$21.95**

FINDING JOY
A Practical Spiritual Guide to Happiness
by *Dannel I. Schwartz* with *Mark Hass*

Searching for happiness in our modern world of stress and struggle is common; *finding* it is more unusual. This guide explores and explains how to find joy through a time-honored, creative—and surprisingly practical—approach based on the teachings of Jewish mysticism and Kabbalah.

"Lovely, simple introduction to Kabbalah....a singular contribution...."
—*American Library Association's* Booklist

•AWARD WINNER•
6" x 9", 192 pp. Quality PB, ISBN 1-58023-009-1 **$14.95** HC, ISBN 1-879045-53-2 **$19.95**

THE DEATH OF DEATH
Resurrection and Immortality in Jewish Thought
by *Neil Gillman*

Explores the original and compelling argument that Judaism, a religion often thought to pay little attention to the afterlife, not only offers us rich ideas on the subject—but delivers a deathblow to death itself.

6" x 9", 336 pp., HC, ISBN 1-879045-61-3 **$23.95**

THE EMPTY CHAIR: FINDING HOPE & JOY
Timeless Wisdom from a Hasidic Master,
Rebbe Nachman of Breslov
Adapted by *Moshe Mykoff* and the *Breslov Research Institute*

A "little treasure" of aphorisms and advice for living joyously and spiritually today, written 200 years ago, but startlingly fresh in meaning and use. Teacher, guide and spiritual master—Rebbe Nachman provides vital words of inspiration and wisdom for life today for people of any faith, or of no faith.

•AWARD WINNER•   "For anyone of any faith, this is a book of healing and wholeness, of being alive!"
— *Bookviews*
4" x 6", 128 pp., 2-color text, Deluxe Paperback, ISBN 1-879045-67-2 **$9.95**

THE GENTLE WEAPON
Prayers for Everyday and Not-So-Everyday Moments
Adapted by *Moshe Mykoff* and *S.C. Mizrahi*,
together with the *Breslov Research Institute*

A small treasury of prayers for people of all faiths, based on the Jewish wisdom tradition. The perfect companion to *The Empty Chair: Finding Hope and Joy*, and to our stressful lives.

4" x 6", 144 pp., 2-color text, Deluxe Paperback, ISBN 1-58023-022-9 **$9.95**

Theology/Philosophy

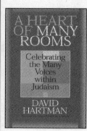

A HEART OF MANY ROOMS
Celebrating the Many Voices within Judaism
by *David Hartman*

With clarity, passion and outstanding scholarship, David Hartman addresses the spiritual and theological questions that face all Jews and all people today. From the perspective of traditional Judaism, he helps us understand the varieties of 20th-century Jewish practice and shows that commitment to both Jewish tradition and to pluralism can create bridges of understanding between people of different religious convictions.

"An extraordinary book, devoid of stereotypic thinking; lucid and pertinent, a modern classic."
—*Michael Walzer, Institute for Advanced Study, Princeton*

6" x 9", 352 pp. HC, ISBN 1-58023-048-2 **$24.95**

WINNER,
National Jewish
Book Award

A LIVING COVENANT
The Innovative Spirit in Traditional Judaism
by *David Hartman*

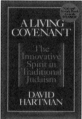

The Judaic tradition is often seen as being more concerned with uncritical obedience to law than with individual freedom and responsibility. Hartman challenges this approach by revealing a Judaism grounded in a covenant—a relational framework—informed by the metaphor of marital love rather than that of parent-child dependency.

"Jews and non-Jews, liberals and traditionalists will see classic Judaism anew in these pages."
—*Dr. Eugene B. Borowitz,*
Hebrew Union College–Jewish Institute of Religion

•AWARD WINNER•

6" x 9", 368 pp. Quality Paperback, ISBN 1-58023-011-3 **$18.95**

• CLASSICS BY ABRAHAM JOSHUA HESCHEL •

The Earth Is the Lord's: The Inner World of the Jew in Eastern Europe
5½" x 8", 112 pp, Quality Paperback, ISBN 1-879045-42-7 **$13.95**

Israel: An Echo of Eternity with new Introduction by Susannah Heschel
5½" x 8", 272 pp, Quality Paperback, ISBN 1-879045-70-2 **$18.95**

A Passion for Truth: Despair and Hope in Hasidism
5½" x 8", 352 pp, Quality Paperback, ISBN 1-879045-41-9 **$18.95**

• THEOLOGY & PHILOSOPHY…Other books•

Aspects of Rabbinic Theology by Solomon Schechter, with a new Introduction by Neil Gillman 6" x 9", 440 pp, Quality Paperback, ISBN 1-879045-24-9 **$18.95**

The Last Trial: On the Legends and Lore of the Command to Abraham to Offer Isaac as a Sacrifice by Shalom Spiegel, with a new Introduction by Judah Goldin
6" x 9", 208 pp, Quality Paperback, ISBN 1-879045-29-X **$17.95**

Judaism and Modern Man: An Interpretation of Jewish Religion by Will Herberg; new Introduction by Neil Gillman 5½" x 8½", 336 pp, Quality Paperback, ISBN 1-879045-87-7 **$18.95**

Seeking the Path to Life: Theological Meditations On God and the Nature of People, Love, Life and Death by Rabbi Ira F. Stone
6" x 9", 132 pp, Quality Paperback, ISBN 1-879045-47-8 **$14.95**; HC, ISBN 1-879045-17-6 **$19.95**

The Spirit of Renewal: Finding Faith After the Holocaust by Edward Feld
6" x 9", 224 pp, Quality Paperback, ISBN 1-879045-40-0 **$16.95**

Tormented Master: The Life and Spiritual Quest of Rabbi Nahman of Bratslav by Arthur Green 6" x 9", 408 pp, Quality Paperback, ISBN 1-879045-11-7 **$18.95**

Your Word Is Fire Ed. and trans. with a new Introduction by Arthur Green and Barry W. Holtz 6" x 9", 152 pp, Quality Paperback, ISBN 1-879045-25-7 **$14.95**

Healing/Recovery/Wellness

Experts Praise *Twelve Jewish Steps to Recovery*

"Recommended reading for people of all denominations."
—*Rabbi Abraham J. Twerski, M.D.*

TWELVE JEWISH STEPS TO RECOVERY
A Personal Guide to Turning from Alcoholism & Other Addictions...Drugs, Food, Gambling, Sex...
by *Rabbi Kerry M. Olitzky & Stuart A. Copans, M.D.*
Preface by *Abraham J. Twerski, M.D.*; Intro. by *Rabbi Sheldon Zimmerman*; "Getting Help" by *JACS Foundation*

A Jewish perspective on the Twelve Steps of addiction recovery programs with consolation, inspiration and motivation for recovery. It draws from traditional sources and quotes from what recovering Jewish people say about their experiences with addictions of all kinds. Inspiring illustrations of the twelve gates of the Old City of Jerusalem introduce each step.

6" x 9", 136 pp. Quality Paperback, ISBN 1-879045-09-5 **$13.95**

Recovery from Codependence: A Jewish Twelve Steps Guide to Healing Your Soul
by Rabbi Kerry M. Olitzky
6" x 9", 160 pp. Quality Paperback Original, ISBN 1-879045-32-X **$13.95**; HC, ISBN -27-3 **$21.95**

Renewed Each Day: Daily Twelve Step Recovery Meditations Based on the Bible
by Rabbi Kerry M. Olitzky & Aaron Z.
6" x 9", Quality Paperback Original **V. I**, 224 pp., ISBN 1-879045-12-5 **$14.95**
V. II, 280 pp., ISBN 1-879045-13-3 **$16.95**

One Hundred Blessings Every Day: Daily Twelve Step Recovery Affirmations, Exercises for Personal Growth & Renewal Reflecting Seasons of the Jewish Year
by Rabbi Kerry M. Olitzky
4½" x 6½", 432 pp. Quality Paperback Original, ISBN 1-879045-30-3 **$14.95**

HEALING OF SOUL, HEALING OF BODY
Spiritual Leaders Unfold the Strength and Solace in Psalms
Edited by *Rabbi Simkha Y. Weintraub, CSW, for The Jewish Healing Center*

A source of solace for those who are facing illness, as well as those who care for them. The ten Psalms which form the core of this healing resource were originally selected 200 years ago by Rabbi Nachman of Breslov as a "complete remedy." Today, for anyone coping with illness, they continue to provide a wellspring of strength. Each Psalm is newly translated, making it clear and accessible, and each one is introduced by an eminent rabbi, men and women reflecting different movements and backgrounds. To all who are living with the pain and uncertainty of illness, this spiritual resource offers an anchor of spiritual comfort.

"Will bring comfort to anyone fortunate enough to read it. This gentle book is
a luminous gem of wisdom."
—*Larry Dossey, M.D., author of* Healing Words: The Power
of Prayer & the Practice of Medicine

6" x 9", 128 pp. Quality Paperback Original, illus., 2-color text, ISBN 1-879045-31-1 **$14.95**

Life Cycle

GRIEF IN OUR SEASONS
A Mourner's Kaddish Companion
by *Rabbi Kerry M. Olitzky*

Strength from the Jewish tradition for the first year of mourning.

Provides a wise and inspiring selection of sacred Jewish writings and a simple, powerful ancient ritual for mourners to read each day, to help hold the memory of their loved ones in their hearts. It offers a comforting, step-by-step daily link to saying *Kaddish*.

"A hopeful, compassionate guide along the journey from grief to rebirth from mourning to a new morning."
—*Rabbi Levi Meier, Ph.D., Chaplain, Cedars–Sinai Medical Center, Los Angeles*

4½" x 6½", 448 pp. Quality Paperback Original, ISBN 1-879045-55-9 **$15.95**

MOURNING & MITZVAH
A Guided Journal for Walking the Mourner's Path Through Grief to Healing

• WITH OVER 60 GUIDED EXERCISES •

by *Anne Brener, L.C.S.W.*
Foreword by *Rabbi Jack Riemer*; Introduction by *Rabbi William Cutter*

"Fully engaging in mourning means you will be a different person than before you began." **For those who mourn a death, for those who would help them,** for those who face a loss of any kind, Brener teaches us the power and strength available to us in the fully experienced mourning process. Guided writing exercises help stimulate the processes of both conscious and unconscious healing.

"A stunning book! It offers an exploration in depth of the place where psychology and religious ritual intersect, and the name of that place is Truth."
—*Rabbi Harold Kushner, author of* When Bad Things Happen to Good People

7½" x 9", 288 pp. Quality Paperback Original, ISBN 1-879045-23-0 **$19.95**

A TIME TO MOURN, A TIME TO COMFORT
A Guide to Jewish Bereavement and Comfort
by *Dr. Ron Wolfson*

A guide to meeting the needs of those who mourn and those who seek to provide comfort in times of sadness. While this book is written from a layperson's point of view, it also includes the specifics for funeral preparations and practical guidance for preparing the home and family to sit *shiva*.

"A sensitive and perceptive guide to Jewish tradition. Both those who mourn and those who comfort will find it a map to accompany them through the whirlwind."
—*Deborah E. Lipstadt, Emory University*

7" x 9", 336 pp. Quality Paperback, ISBN 1-879045-96-6 **$16.95**

WHEN A GRANDPARENT DIES
A Kid's Own Remembering Workbook for Dealing with Shiva and the Year Beyond
by *Nechama Liss-Levinson, Ph.D.*

Drawing insights from both psychology and Jewish tradition, this workbook helps children participate in the process of mourning, offering guided exercises, rituals, and places to write, draw, list, create and express their feelings.

"Will bring support, guidance, and understanding for countless children, teachers, and health professionals."
—*Rabbi Earl A. Grollman, D.D., author of* Talking about Death

8" x 10", 48 pp. HC, illus., 2-color text, ISBN 1-879045-44-3 **$15.95**

Life Cycle

TEARS OF SORROW, SEEDS OF HOPE
A Jewish Spiritual Companion for Infertility and Pregnancy Loss
by *Rabbi Nina Beth Cardin*

Many people who endure the emotional suffering of infertility, pregnancy loss, or stillbirth bear this sorrow alone. Rarely is the experience of loss and infertility discussed with anyone but close friends and family members. Despite the private nature of the pain, many women and men would welcome the opportunity to be comforted by family and a community who would understand the pain and loneliness they feel, and the emptiness caused by the loss that is without a face, a name, or a grave.

Tears of Sorrow, Seeds of Hope is a spiritual companion that enables us to mourn infertility, a lost pregnancy, or a stillbirth within the prayers, rituals, and meditation of Judaism. By drawing deeply on the texts of tradition, it creates readings and rites of mourning, and through them provides a wellspring of compassion, solace—and hope.

6" x 9", 192 pp. HC, ISBN 1-58023-017-2 **$19.95**

•AWARD WINNER•

LIFECYCLES
V. 1: Jewish Women on Life Passages & Personal Milestones
Edited and with Introductions by *Rabbi Debra Orenstein*
V. 2: Jewish Women on Biblical Themes in Contemporary Life
Edited and with Introductions by
Rabbi Debra Orenstein and *Rabbi Jane Rachel Litman*

This unique multivolume collaboration brings together over one hundred women writers, rabbis, and scholars to create the first comprehensive work on Jewish life cycle that fully includes women's perspectives.

V. 1: 6" x 9", 480 pp. Quality Paperback, ISBN 1-58023-018-0 **$19.95**
HC, ISBN 1-879045-14-1 **$24.95**
V. 2: 6" x 9", 464 pp. Quality Paperback, ISBN 1-58023-019-9 **$19.95**
HC, ISBN 1-879045-15-X **$24.95**

LIFE CYCLE— The Art of Jewish Living Series for Holiday Observance
by Dr. Ron Wolfson

Hanukkah—7" x 9", 192 pp. Quality Paperback, ISBN 1-879045-97-4 **$16.95**

The Shabbat Seder—7" x 9", 272 pp. Quality Paperback, ISBN 1-879045-90-7 **$16.95**;
Booklet of Blessings **$5.00**; Audiocassette of Blessings **$6.00**; Teacher's Guide **$4.95**

The Passover Seder—7" x 9", 336 pp. Quality Paperback, ISBN 1-879045-93-1 **$16.95**;
Passover Workbook, **$6.95**; Audiocassette of Blessings, **$6.00**; Teacher's Guide, **$4.95**

• LIFE CYCLE...Other Books •

A Heart of Wisdom: Making the Jewish Journey from Midlife Through the Elder Years
Ed. by Susan Berrin 6" x 9", 384 pp. Quality Paperback, ISBN 1-58023-051-2, **$18.95**;
HC, ISBN 1-879045-73-7 **$24.95**

Bar/Bat Mitzvah Basics: A Practical Family Guide to Coming of Age Together
Ed. by Cantor Helen Leneman 6" x 9", 240 pp. Quality Paperback, ISBN 1-879045-54-0 **$16.95**

Embracing the Covenant: Converts to Judaism Talk About Why & How
Ed. and with Intros. by Rabbi Allan L. Berkowitz and Patti Moskovitz
6" x 9", 192 pp. Quality Paperback, ISBN 1-879045-50-8 **$15.95**

For Kids—Putting God on Your Guest List: How to Claim the Spiritual Meaning of Your Bar or Bat Mitzvah by Rabbi Jeffrey K. Salkin
6" x 9", 144 pp. Quality Paperback Original, ISBN 1-58023-015-6 **$14.95**

The New Jewish Baby Book: Names, Ceremonies, Customs—A Guide for Today's Families by Anita Diamant 6" x 9", 336 pp. Quality Paperback, ISBN 1-879045-28-1 **$16.95**

Putting God on the Guest List, 2nd Ed.: How to Reclaim the Spiritual Meaning of Your Child's Bar or Bat Mitzvah by Rabbi Jeffrey K. Salkin
6" x 9", 224 pp. Quality Paperback, ISBN 1-897045-59-1 **$16.95**; HC, ISBN 1-879045-58-3 **$24.95**

So That Your Values Live On: Ethical Wills & How to Prepare Them
Ed. by Rabbi Jack Riemer & Professor Nathaniel Stampfer
6" x 9", 272 pp. Quality Paperback, ISBN 1-879045-34-6 **$17.95**

Children's Spirituality

A PRAYER FOR THE EARTH
The Story of Naamah, Noah's Wife

For ages 4 and up

by *Sandy Eisenberg Sasso*
Full-color illustrations by *Bethanne Andersen*

NONDENOMINATIONAL, NONSECTARIAN

This new story, based on an ancient text, opens readers' religious imaginations to new ideas about the well-known story of the Flood. When God tells Noah to bring the animals of the world onto the ark, God *also* calls on Naamah, Noah's wife, to save each plant on Earth.

> "A lovely tale....Children of all ages should be drawn to this parable for our times."
> —*Tomie dePaola, artist/author of books for children*

•AWARD WINNER•

9" x 12", 32 pp. HC, Full-color illus., ISBN 1-879045-60-5 **$16.95**

THE 11TH COMMANDMENT
Wisdom from Our Children   **For all ages**
by The Children of America

MULTICULTURAL, NONDENOMINATIONAL, NONSECTARIAN

"If there were an Eleventh Commandment, what would it be?"

Children of many religious denominations across America answer this question—in their own drawings and words—in *The 11th Commandment*.

> "Wonderful....This unusual book provides both food for thought and insight into the hopes and fears of today's young."
> —*American Library Association's* Booklist

8" x 10", 48 pp. HC, Full-color illus., ISBN 1-879045-46-X **$16.95**

SHARING BLESSINGS
Children's Stories for Exploring the Spirit of the Jewish Holidays

For ages 6 and up

by *Rahel Musleah* and *Rabbi Michael Klayman*
Full-color illustrations by *Mary O'Keefe Young*

What is the spiritual message of each of the Jewish holidays?
How do we teach it to our children?

Many books tell children about the historical significance and customs of the holidays. Now, through engaging, creative stories about one family's spiritual preparation, *Sharing Blessings* explores ways to get into the *spirit* of 13 different holidays.

> "A beguiling introduction to important Jewish values by way of the holidays."
> —*Rabbi Harold Kushner, author of* When Bad Things Happen to Good People *and* How Good Do We Have to Be?

7" x 10", 64 pp. HC, Full-color illus., ISBN 1-879045-71-0 **$18.95**

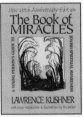

THE BOOK OF MIRACLES   **For ages 9–13**
A Young Person's Guide to Jewish Spiritual Awareness
by *Lawrence Kushner*

With a Special 10th Anniversary Introduction and all new illustrations by the author.

From the miracle at the Red Sea to the miracle of waking up this morning, this intriguing book introduces kids to a way of everyday spiritual thinking to last a lifetime. Kushner, whose award-winning books have brought spirituality to life for countless adults, now shows young people how to use Judaism as a foundation on which to build their lives.

6" x 9", 96 pp. HC, 2-color illus., ISBN 1-879045-78-8 **$16.95**

Children's Spirituality

For ages 8 and up

BUT GOD REMEMBERED
Stories of Women from Creation to the Promised Land
by *Sandy Eisenberg Sasso*, Full-color illus. by *Bethanne Andersen*

NONDENOMINATIONAL, NONSECTARIAN

A fascinating collection of four different stories of women only briefly mentioned in biblical tradition and religious texts, but never before explored. Award-winning author Sasso brings to life the intriguing stories of Lilith, Serach, Bityah, and the Daughters of Z, courageous and strong women from ancient tradition. All teach important values through their faith and actions.

9" x 12", 32 pp. HC, Full-color illus., ISBN 1-879045-43-5 **$16.95**

•AWARD WINNER•

IN GOD'S NAME
by *Sandy Eisenberg Sasso*

For ages 4 and up

Selected as Outstanding by Parent Council, Ltd.™

Full-color illustrations by *Phoebe Stone*

MULTICULTURAL, NONDENOMINATIONAL, NONSECTARIAN

Like an ancient myth in its poetic text and vibrant illustrations, this modern fable about the search for God's name celebrates the diversity and, at the same time, the unity of all the people of the world. Each seeker claims he or she alone knows the answer. Finally, they come together and learn what God's name really is, sharing the ultimate harmony of belief in one God by people of all faiths, all backgrounds.

•AWARD WINNER•

9" x 12", 32 pp. HC, Full color illus., ISBN 1-879045-26-5 **$16.95**

For ages 4 and up

GOD IN BETWEEN
by *Sandy Eisenberg Sasso*
Full-color illustrations by *Sally Sweetland*

NONDENOMINATIONAL, NONSECTARIAN, MULTICULTURAL

If you wanted to find God, where would you look?

A magical, mythical tale that teaches that God can be found where we are: within all of us and the relationships between us.

9" x 12", 32 pp. HC, Full-color illus., ISBN 1-879045-86-9 **$16.95**

IN OUR IMAGE
God's First Creatures

For ages 4 and up

Selected as Outstanding by Parent Council, Ltd.™

by *Nancy Sohn Swartz*
Full-color illustrations by *Melanie Hall*
NONDENOMINATIONAL, NONSECTARIAN
For ages 4 and up

A playful new twist to the Creation story. Celebrates the interconnectedness of nature and the harmony of all living things.

9" x 12", 32 pp. HC, Full-color illus., ISBN 1-879045-99-0 **$16.95**

•AWARD WINNER•

•AWARD WINNER•

For ages 4 and up

GOD'S PAINTBRUSH
by *Sandy Eisenberg Sasso*
Full-color illustrations by *Annette Compton*

MULTICULTURAL, NONDENOMINATIONAL, NONSECTARIAN

Invites children of all faiths and backgrounds to encounter God openly in their own lives. Wonderfully interactive, provides questions adult and child can explore together at the end of each episode.

11" x 8½", 32 pp. HC, Full-color illus., ISBN 1-879045-22-2 **$16.95**

Also Available! **Teacher's Guide: A Guide for Jewish & Christian Educators and Parents**

8½" x 11", 32 pp. PB, ISBN 1-879045-57-5 **$6.95**

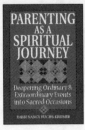